AF615694

I Would've Been A Lumberjack

(But I Couldn't Hack It)

by

Van Craddock

Larry
Here's wishing you big success
on your newest endeavor!
Hope you enjoy the book.
Van Craddock

I Would've Been A Lumberjack

(But I Couldn't Hack It)

ISBN 1-878096-21-4

First Printing, 1991

Best of East Texas Publishers
515 South First • P.O. Box 1647
Lufkin, Texas 75901
(409) 634-7444

Dedication

To Better Half, Bozo and Bright Eyes
(Bettye, Chris and Cathy)

FOREWORD

All right, Mom. OK, David. You too, Helen.

For you seven or eight folks who, down through the years, have said, "Why don't you publish a book of your columns?" – well, here it is.

What you'll find inside is a collection of some of the 1,300 columns (give or take a couple) written for the Longview News-Journal since September 1978.

I've tried to pick a range of subjects that would be representative of my column through the years. That means you'll find some humor (yes, even puns), a little East Texas history, some musings about life in general.

And, of course, there are columns about Better Half, Bozo and Bright Eyes, who surely must be the best sports in the world to let me continue writing about them the way I do.

I have former News-Journal Publisher Margaret Estes Davis and Joe Calvit to thank (others might use the phrase "to blame") for the opportunity to pen a twice-weekly column for the News-Journal. Joe, who was my managing editor at the time, wandered over to my desk one day and asked if I'd like to try my hand at a column. Naturally, I jumped at the chance and have been doing it ever since.

Writing the column has been a real joy – except for those times that writer's block set in as the copy deadline approached. I'm glad to say those times have come infrequently since there usually has been plenty to write about.

Newspapering is a lot like a disease. Once you get printer's ink in your veins, it's awfully hard to get it out. I'd be remiss if I didn't say "thank you" to two people who, more than anyone else, instilled in me a love of journalism. They were Ben Hobbs and the late Dr. Francine Hoffman (you'll find a column about Dr. Hoffman in the book), both from Stephen F. Austin State University in Nacogdoches.

Better Half and I spent many a late night in old Birdwell Annex at SFA, working with Dr. H and "Gentle Ben" to help put to bed the next issue of the school paper, The Pine Log. They were wonderful instructors, and this book is dedicated to them, too.

Finally, many, many thanks to Publisher Retta Kelley and the Longview News-Journal for permission to put together a collection like this.

I hope you enjoy the book.

Van Craddock
Longview, Texas

Table Of Contents

1

A Place That Feels Like Home

If you have to be buried, I can't think of a better place than this.

The country cemetery is in the middle of nowhere, and that's the beauty of it. It sits far from town, at the end of a dirt trail off a farm-to-market road, in a grove of oak trees nestled behind the prettiest little white frame Presbyterian church you ever saw.

I don't get up this way as often as I'd like. It's about 100 miles from Longview, just this side of Oklahoma. But when I do make it up here, I feel like I'm at home.

A couple of rain drops landed on the windshield as I stopped the car by the cemetery's front gate. From the way the wind was picking up, it looked like we were about to get a gullywasher.

My grandparents are buried here. So are my great-grandparents and a bunch of other relatives. I can put faces with some of the names on the grave markers, but other names I only know from conversations and family Bibles.

I don't mean to sound morbid, but cemeteries are fascinating places. There's so much history in graveyards. And where relatives are concerned, they bring back a lot of memories, too.

Standing beside my grandparents' graves, I remembered the summer days I'd spent up here as a little boy. They had this big old dog named Sport, and Sport and I would spend hours roaming in the woods behind their house.

My grandfather would take me bird hunting, and sometimes we'd go down to city hall where he served as city clerk. Once, I remember him introducing me to the mayor. I was probably 6 at the time, and was I impressed!

My grandmother was always cooking up something good for me to eat. Even better, she thought I was perfect and could do no wrong. Everybody needs at least one grandmother like that.

Back in the car, I was just pulling away from the cemetery when the bottom dropped out. It started raining good and hard.

Coming up here also gave me an excuse to visit Aunt Ruth. She lives about 20 minutes from the cemetery, in the next little town down the road.

If you don't have an Aunt Ruth, you should. She's my dad's sister and one of the most unselfish people I've ever known, always doing for others.

"Oh shoot!" she said, surprised to find it was me standing in the rain knocking on her back door.

By the time I was seated at the kitchen table, she'd set down a saucer of pecan pie and a diet Dr Pepper and was apologizing because she didn't have anything else to offer.

I'd fixed you a ham sandwich if I had any ham," she said.

Aunt Ruth had some health problems a while back, but she'd be the last one to complain about it. She did admit, however, to having a hard time shaking a cold. "And I've got a touch of the jakeleg," she said, smiling and patting her knee. "But when you get my age, I don't guess that's so bad."

For the next 30 minutes, we caught up on aunts and uncles and cousins from California to North Carolina.

"I want you to pick out a painting before you leave," she said. She's a painter, and she loves to do bluebonnets and country scenes and such. She's good, too.

I told her I couldn't take one of her paintings. Besides, I said, I was afraid it'd get wet taking it to the car. It was raining even harder now.

"Oh law," she said, "I don't mean now. I mean when I'm gone!" So I picked a painting of a barn she'd done in 1979. It was Alvin's barn, she said. Alvin was her late husband, and she still misses him very much. She asked for one of my business cards, and she taped it to the back of the painting so people would know who has dibs on it.

It's a really nice painting, and I'll be proud to own it. But I hope I don't get it for a long, long time.

(October 15, 1989)

2

Just can't explain journalism's appeal

"What made you decide to get into journalism?" That's a question I get asked occasionally. In fact, even my boss has asked me that question a time or two.

I suppose there are a couple of reasons I decided on newspaper work. Aside from the obvious big bucks that all journalists make, the thing I probably enjoy most about newspapering is the fact it's never dull.

For instance, what other job could you have where you'd get the chance to interview John Connally in an airport restroom? I did that once, although I'm sure when I'm old and gray my grandkids will never believe me.

Or where else could you sit down with somebody like the great English writer/philosopher Malcolm Muggeridge and discuss life, death and religion for an hour? (When the 80-year-old Muggeridge was in Longview for a speaking engagement several years ago, he said, "The media are great fun if you don't take anything they do seriously.").

Then there was the time we heard a police radio report of a possible hostage situation in a downtown office building. "Man may have a gun," the radio crackled. So an editor, a photographer and yours truly raced down the street and took an elevator to the top floor, not knowing what to expect when the door opened.

Barging blindly into a possibly very ticklish situation had seemed like the thing to do at the time, but when we got back to the office we started thinking how stupid we'd been. "We could have all been blown away," the photographer said, and he was right, too.

As I said, this job is never boring. It's not an easy job, either, although anybody who ever watched "Lou Grant" would probably disagree. It always bothered me that Billie and Joe Rossi never seemed to have any deadlines on the show. "When do you need the story, boss?" Billie would say. "Oh, take as much time as you need, Billie," Lou'd reply. "Three, four months maybe."

In truth, deadlines are unbending, the daily albatross around the journalist's neck. It was Red Smith, the great sportswriter, who probably summed it up best. "Oh, writing is simple," Smith once said. "All you do is sit in front of a typewriter until you sweat blood."

It certainly wasn't an easy profession back in 1849 when my great-great uncle hauled an ox cart full of printing equipment to the banks of the Trinity River in 1849 to found Dallas' first newspaper, the Dallas Herald. I think journalists were more respected back then, though.

A survey done a while back on Americans' trust in various professions showed journalists ranked in the middle of the pack. We were tied with morticians, well behind physicians but ahead of used car salesmen. Oh well.

I especially like what Stanley Walker had to say about the profession. Walker was city editor for the old New York Herald-Tribune, and he wrote this in 1934:

"What makes good newspapermen? The answer is easy. They know everything. They are aware not only of what goes on in the world today but their brains are repositories of the accumulated wisdom of the ages.

"They are not only handsome, but they have the physical strength which enables them to perform great feats of energy. They can go for nights on end without sleep. They dress well and talk with charm. Men and women admire and adore them; tycoons and statesmen are willing to share their secrets with them.

"They hate lies and meanness and sham, but keep their temper. They are loyal to their paper and to what they look upon as their profession whether it is a profession or merely a craft; they resent attempts to debase it.

"When they die, a lot of people are sorry, and some remember them for several days."

(March 9, 1984)

3

Bouncing newspaperman has had a ball

No, I haven't always been in newspaper work. One of my first jobs was selling bowling balls door to door, but I found out that wasn't down my alley.

When I was younger I thought I wanted to be a plumber, but that was only a pipe dream. I hired on as a ditch digger after high school, but found myself in a rut.

Why, for a brief period I even worked at a casket factory, but decided the job was just too laid back. SWEPCO wouldn't let me be a pole climber, either, because they said I was too high strung. Then there were a few months when I was a painter, but they let me go because I was making too many off-color remarks.

Being a patriotic type, I trained to be a covert explosives expert for the CIA, but one day I blew my cover. As you can see, nothing seemed to work out. I tried to join the electricians' union, but they told me there was nothing current. Sold scotch tape and that didn't stick. Was briefly a trailer salesman but there were too many hitches, and down on the coast worked in a sardine factory until I got canned.

In college I majored in changing my major. I really wanted to be a teacher but was told I had no class. For a while I thought about accounting, until the dean said I was no account.

Turned to archaeology and didn't dig it. I tried history as a major but kept repeating myself, then transferred to Stephen F. Austin State University as a forestry major but found myself out on a limb (I just couldn't hack it as a lumberjack).

Somebody suggested I look into law school, but as a lawyer I figured everybody would be on my case. At one point I bought several expensive cameras and went into photography, but nothing developed out of that. Then my parents said I should go into the ministry, but somehow I knew nobody would appreciate my altar ego.

Despite the setbacks, I kept plugging away. Being a sports-minded person I tried out for the St. Louis Cardinals but it just wasn't in the Cards. Undaunted, I went to the Houston Astros who quickly told me I had three strikes against me. As a pro golfer I wasn't up to par.

It was then that I decided to become a physician. Unfortunately I flunked out of medical school (they insisted I didn't have enough patience). I didn't have enough pull to become a dentist, so I tried my hand at faith-healing but it made me sick. Once I sneaked into a hospital and pretended I was an X-ray technician, but they saw right through me.

As a red-blooded American I considered being a full-time blood donor, but would you believe the blood bank said I wasn't their type?

I continued to go from this to that. Operated an elevator until they showed me the door. Worked in a reducing salon until the owners decided to trim the fat. Hired on as a guide at a national park, but was finally sent packing. Worked at a grocery store but was sacked. Even wanted to be an animal-control officer, but the city told me I wasn't dogged enough.

Being a carpenter didn't hit the nail on the head, and briefly attempted to be a meteorologist but was always under the weather. It was then I decided to go into business for myself.

I opened a tuxedo rental shop and that didn't suit me. Had a clock repair shop but naturally had too much time on my hands. Thought I'd make a real cleaning with my own laundry, too, but quickly found myself washed up.

Desperate, it was then I considered turning to some things I shouldn't have. I hate to admit this, but I even thought about joining the KKK (until I found it too clanish). Why, I even settled in a nudist colony, but I just couldn't bare it.

Yep, it took a while before I found my niche in journalism. I've enjoyed newspaper work, too, but one of these days I just might try something else.

I'm leaning toward becoming a judge, but right now I just don't seem to be able to reach a decision.

(September 2, 1981)

4

The president got his possum

This is the tale of President William Howard Taft and the possum and 'tater dinner he got in Longview in 1909.

Taft was president between Roosevelt and Wilson, but he's probably best remembered for weighing 325 pounds and once getting stuck in his White House bathtub. He had this enormous appetite, see, and often ate steak for breakfast. But in October 1909, the chief executive had possums on his mind.

Elected in 1908, Republican Taft was touring Texas (a state he lost by a wide margin to popular Democrat William Jennings Bryan) and receiving big receptions in Houston, Waco and Dallas. But it was in the Waller County town of Hempstead that somebody gave him a live possum and suggested it would make a delicious meal.

Well, the Yale-educated president quickly admitted to having an "aversion to the possum fad" and announced he would probably stick with steak. Possum was just too hard to, er, stomach.

Anyway, on Oct. 24, 1909, Taft boarded his "Mayflower" special train at the Dallas depot and headed east. A few miles out of town the president had a change of heart and decided, by golly, that he'd just try that possum out.

But when the train's chef went to the baggage car to get the possum, he discovered that apparently someone in Dallas had swiped the animal, cage and all.

Now this would never do! Here the president of these United States wanted possum for lunch, and the fool critter had disappeared. So while the train stopped in Wills Point, the train's crew and several of the presidential party (including Secretary of War Jacob McGavock Dickinson) set about looking for the missing possum. But he was long gone.

Just before noon, the "Mayflower" pulled into the depot in

downtown Longview. Now, it isn't every day that a U.S. president comes to town, and Longview rolled out the red carpet. According to contemporary reports, a crowd of 5,000 to 6,000 (that was everybody in Longview in 1909) assembled on the public square to see and hear Taft, whose stomach was probably beginning to growl by now.

"The president was introduced by Mayor G.A. Bodenheim, who tendered the freedom of the city and the welcome of East Texas," read one newspaper account.

Taft thanked the mayor for his kindness and told the crowd he'd wanted to stop in Longview because it was the home of an acquaintance, Texas Gov. Thomas M. Campbell. Speaking in a "hoarse and sore" throat, the president cracked a joke about having heard the governor had "moved to the promised land — Palestine."

Taft seemed pleased with the elaborate decorations made by residents for the occasion, especially the 25-foot-tall triumphal arch covered with bunting and flags and carrying the message "WELCOME."

"Ropes separated ladies, gentlemen and negroes in three sections," a newspaper article said, and Taft, who admitted he'd found "more friends and less votes" in Texas than any other state, was cheered lustily by his audience.

And then it happened. Out of the crowd came a resident identified as one Cooper Sheftall, and guess what ol' Cooper was carrying in his hands? Yep. A possum and 'tater dinner, ready to be consumed by the president.

Maybe word of the missing possum had reached Longview, or maybe it was just coincidence. Whatever the reason, the president of the United States got his first taste of possum in Longview, Texas.

The presidential train traveled on to Marshall, where Taft spoke to another large audience while the engine took on water. Later that afternoon another 3,000 persons also gathered at Jefferson to see the president, but the train didn't stop and few in the crowd got to see Taft because he appeared late at the rear door of the train. Maybe he was busy finishing up his possum dinner.

But we can be sure of one thing, and that's the fact that William Howard Taft left East Texas with a good taste in his mouth.

(June 24, 1981)

5

Never ever joke with a woman in labor

Anyone who doesn't believe in miracles apparently has never been in a hospital delivery room.

Sunday night I watched the miracle of birth, and I'm still on a natural high. It was one of the grandest experiences of my life.

Good Shepherd Hospital didn't allow husbands in the delivery room when Bozo was born three years ago. But the Age of Enlightenment finally dawned and that's changed now. This time I wanted to be where the action was, so to speak.

Oh sure, I had some doubts at first. I'd heard stories about fainting hubbys and all that. But Better Half and I signed up for the hospital's childbirth classes (husbands have to take the class if they want to be in the delivery room), and the farther we got into the class the more I knew I wanted to be with Better Half.

The classes met once a week for six weeks, and it covered topics ranging from fetal development and exercises to drugs and breathing techniques. There were about 15 couples in our group, and I've never seen so many pregnant women in one place in my whole life.

We saw films and discussed the childbirth process and toured the delivery rooms and OB, and at the end we even got a certificate for our "graduation."

It's a great course, whether you're planning to be in the delivery room with your wife or not, and well worth the money.

Having just experienced the birth of a second child, I've determined there are three basic laws of nature where childbirth is concerned:

(1) Babies are never born at a decent hour.

(2) No matter how much planning you do (suitcases packed, quarters collected for calling relatives, etc.), you're never really

ready when it happens.

(3) Never — but never — joke with a woman who's in labor.

Having contractions late Sunday night means a logistics problem if you've got a 3-year-old. Thankfully, a neighbor was more than happy to stay with Bozo (sound asleep during all the activity) while we grabbed our bags and headed for the emergency room.

It was apparent the youngster wasn't going to wait too long to arrive, so Better Half was wheeled up to OB while an anxious husband tagged along behind.

While she was placed in a labor room, I donned my hospital greens as fast as I could (although I first put my sanitary shoe covers on backwards). Then, mask in hand, I bolted in doing my best Groucho Marx impression. "What seems to be the problem here?" I said, flicking an imaginary cigar and moving my eyebrows Groucho style.

"This isn't any time for humor," Better Half shouted between contractions, giving me low Marx for my comment.

It was strange, being up there close to midnight, because we were the only ones having a baby that time of night. There wasn't even anyone waiting to deliver, so it was sort of like having the hospital all to ourselves.

Shortly we moved into the delivery room, and I was glad I was there. It certainly beat pacing in a hot, cramped waiting room and, besides, it would have been very lonely in the waiting room. And this was no time to be lonely.

And after all, I was there when Better Half got pregnant, you know.

I can tell you that the breathing exercises we learned in our childbirth classes really work. They even worked for me, and I wasn't even pregnant.

We hadn't been in the delivery room more than 10 minutes before the newest family member decided it was finally time to face the world. I just squeezed Better Half's hand in mine, supporting her the best I could during her labor of love.

There's a Jewish proverb that says God couldn't be everywhere, so he made mothers. Watching Better Half hold that tiny little girl in her arms, I decided it must be true.

See, miracles do still happen.

(July 9, 1980)

6

Take time to enjoy the rainbows

Did you see the rainbow the other day?

It just might have been the prettiest rainbow I've ever seen. With colors so vivid they looked like they'd been painted against the sky, it was a complete rainbow, stretching from one side of the horizon to the other.

I must have stared at that rainbow a good five minutes, maybe longer. It was something to behold, and seeing it brought me happiness.

But moments like that are all too rare, I'm afraid.

Most of us are too busy rushing through life to stop and smell the roses — or to enjoy a rainbow. We're all stressed up with no place to go, involved in a rat race the rats are winning.

Happiness, of course, is different things to different people. Mark Twain said it was "good friends, good books and a sleepy conscience." H.L. Mencken insisted the only really happy people in this world "are married women and single men."

But many things — simple things, like rainbows — can bring happiness. For me, they include:

— Discovering that slip of paper on your windshield is an advertising flier, not a parking ticket.

— A leisurely Saturday breakfast, reading the paper and having nowhere to rush to that morning.

—The hummingbird by our kitchen window. For weeks now, he's been visiting our flower bed. He's fascinating to watch and so tiny, and I still don't believe his wings can flap that fast.

— Will Rogers. If I'm feeling down, I pull out my bargain volume of Will's old writings. Funny, but what he wrote more than 50 years ago still applies.

—Singing "Amazing Grace" in church. Shoot, I wouldn't mind if we sang it every week. I think I'd like to have "Amazing Grace" sung at my funeral, but not for a long time, you understand.

— Holding a baby.

— Fireflies. Living in town, we don't see fireflies too often at our house. I remember standing in the back yard of a Tennessee farmhouse years ago, watching hundreds of fireflies dance in the night. It was a wonderful sight.

— Kate Smith belting out "God Bless America." I know. It sounds silly, but I've been known to get all teary eyed when I heard Kate sing that song. I'm the same way when it comes to "Battle Hymn of the Republic" and "Dixie."

— Raking leaves on a crisp fall afternoon.

— Baseball. Bart Giamatti was right. Surely, baseball is God's favorite game.

— Looking for four-leaf clovers. I don't believe we've ever walked down Cargill Long Park without Better Half finding at least one four-leaf clover.

— Watching Bozo hit a double, or Bright Eyes play the piano.

— Texas beating Oklahoma and Arkansas on successive weekends.

— Memories of family reunions. I recall sitting on my grandmother's back porch as a child, paper plate piled high, chewing on a chicken leg and being surrounded by a house full of relatives.

Then all us cousins would play football or check out the cows in the pasture while the grownups talked about the war, pulled out the family albums and compared aches and pains. I didn't know it then, but those were very special times.

Years ago I ran across something titled "How To Be Happy." I don't know who wrote it — I didn't — but it says the way to be happy is to:

"Keep your heart free from hate, your mind free from worry, live simply, give much, sing often, pray always, think of others, and scatter sunshine when you can."

Fact is, Americans are only guaranteed life, liberty and the pursuit of happiness. I think catching up with happiness would be a lot easier if we'd just slow down a little.

Who knows? You might even see a rainbow.

(November 5, 1989)

7

Hoffman tough because she cared

Funny, but everybody had changed except for Francine Hoffman.

Here we were, gathered in the university center, honoring Dr. Hoffman after all these years. Everyone else there had either put on weight or lost hair or added wrinkles, but Dr. H hadn't changed at all.

She still wore her hair in that bun on top of her head, and 14 years after graduation she hadn't aged a day.

Most folks, I suppose, had a teacher in high school or college who had a profound effect on their lives. Mine was Francine Hoffman.

She was a little woman (I'm writing this in past tense like she's died or something, but actually she's only retiring after teaching journalism for a half-century or so). But in class, nobody stood taller. She was, to put it politely, one of those people who could put the fear of God in you.

That's because I generally said a prayer before walking into her classroom.

She held the title of associate professor of journalism and supervisor of student publications when I was attending Stephen F. Austin State University. That meant she had the responsibility of teaching college students how to be journalists.

She always started with the basics. "This, students," she would say, "is a typewriter." But by the time the semester had ended, you either had learned the art of newspapering or you had flunked miserably. There was no in-between.

Francine Hoffman was unswerving in her belief that there was no excuse for sloppy journalism. "Accuracy, accuracy, accuracy," she'd say in class. Typographic errors simply did not appear in the weekly college newspaper we put out. Words were spelled correctly ("Buy you a cheap dictionary," she'd say. "And then make certain you use it.").

All of the headlines fit, and everybody met deadlines. It was as simple as that. She didn't expect us to be perfect, of course. She demanded it.

But she demanded it because she cared. I had some teachers — and you did, too — who simply went through the motions (a lot of students are like that, too, I hasten to add). But not Dr. H. She would accept nothing less than the best.

Some of my fondest memories of SFA (other than the obvious fact I met Better Half in journalism class) are of those late night sessions in old Birdwell Annex, putting together another issue of the paper. It was a marvelous learning experience, a time of camaraderie and a sense of pride in doing the best job we could.

So here we were again, gathered in the university center, saying thanks to Dr. Hoffman. There were a hundred of us, and we had come from Houston and San Antonio and Austin and Oklahoma to let her know how much we'd appreciated her and the fact she cared.

And apparently she had taught her students well. They carried such titles as managing editor and advertising director and city editor, and they represented such newspapers as The Dallas Morning News and the Chicago Sun-Times and the Fort Worth Star Telegram and others, both large and small. Yes, Dr. H had done her job well.

So now she's returning to her home in Wills Point for a well deserved retirement. It's sad to think that so many students won't have the chance to learn under her now. Francine Hoffman was the best.

She cared.

(April 4, 1984)

A very unique city park

Longview, to be sure, has some most unique parks. There's Rotary Park, designed especially for the area's handicapped residents, and the popular, miles-long Cargill Long Park National Recreation Trail that follows an old abandoned railroad bed.

But the most unusual of all the city's park land surely has to be tiny Magrill Plaza near downtown Longview.

Magrill Plaza has the distinction of being owned by a race of people: The land was formally deeded to blacks in the Longview area more than 130 years ago by one John R. Magrill, and the deed remains valid today.

So while the city maintains the 1.5 acres at Green and Padon streets as a park, the city technically doesn't own the land upon which Magrill Plaza sits.

The story of Magrill Plaza goes back as far as the 1850s, when John Magrill, a white man, came to East Texas from Alabama and bought some timber land in Upshur County (Gregg County hadn't yet been created).

In an interview some 30 years ago, C.A. Magrill, a descendant of John Magrill, recalled how the unusual property deed came about.

"There were quite a few Negroes in the area (following the Civil War) and apparently they had no suitable place to worship," he remembered. "Uncle John deeded the land not just to one group, but to all Negroes so they could build what was then known as a meeting house."

The tract, located in a wooded area known as "the groves," quickly proved a popular gathering place for area blacks, some of whom were ex-slaves.

There seems to be some disagreement as to the exact wording of the original deed, which reportedly was destroyed in a courthouse fire in Gilmer many years ago. Some say the land simply was given to East Texas blacks while others say it was transferred to "all persons of African descent in Upshur County."

"If you go by the deed, the property was assigned to the blacks of the Longview area for educational and religious purposes," said W.A. Williams, who is a member of St. Mark Christian Methodist Episcopal Church. The church originated from a brush arbor that was located on the site of present-day Magrill Plaza.

"The (early) church itself was unorganized and non-denominational; more than one religious group worshiped there," Williams said of the Magrill site. Thanks to the deed, he said, permission "was granted for use by blacks socially there. It was a place for them to go rather than to go downtown and sit on the streets."

Down through the years, there have been several attempts — especially during the oil boom of the 1930s — to buy the tract. But it remains as it always has: deeded to the blacks of the community.

"To undo it? I suppose it would take a state court (to overturn the deed)," Williams said. But don't look for anything like that to happen. Everybody seems very satisfied with Magrill Plaza the way it is.

Despite its tiny size, Magrill Plaza just might be the most colorful of Longview's extensive park system. The Longview Men's Garden Club has adopted the park, maintaining its rose garden there, and a beautiful gazebo sits amid the landscaped grounds.

Every Christmas, Magrill becomes home to the city's official "Spirit of Christmas" tree, made of hundreds of red lights strung from the park's flagpole.

But the most colorful thing about Magrill Plaza continues to be its unique history.

(June 8, 1988)

There's nothing like a wedding

I love weddings.

Apparently other people love weddings, too. Why, I know some folks who like weddings so much that they keep getting married every few years. But then, there's a lot of that going on nowadays.

Myself, I never turn down an opportunity to go to a wedding. The bride and groom are beaming at each other and folks are all dressed up and there's pretty music and at the end there's generally a reception with free cake and punch. It's good, cheap entertainment.

Of course, not everybody shares my enthusiasm for attending weddings. Just the other day, for instance, a friend of mine told me he'd had a bad experience at a wedding he went to years ago. "I got married," he said.

I'm not sure if he was teasing or not, but he went on to say that he hasn't been to a wedding in decades. "Not only do I not go to weddings," he said, "but every year I suggest to my wife that to celebrate our anniversary we ought to hang the preacher in effigy." And he wasn't grinning when he said it, either.

Naturally, there are some people who figure they've got something better to do with their time than attend weddings. I had one woman tell me once that her marriage license had only cost $3 when she got married way back when. "Only goes to prove," she said, "that you get what you pay for."

Then there are others who attend weddings who say they're just there to "pray for the groom."

But wild horses couldn't drag me away from a wedding. As a result, I've attended weddings each of the past two weekends — I would have attended a third but I had to work that night — and they were both swell events.

With half of this country's marriages ending in divorce today, it might be a good thing to make it mandatory for married couples to attend a wedding every once in a while. I figure it would be a good way for couples to rekindle some of the spark that may have gone out of their own marriage.

And it's awfully easy, years after a wedding, to let that spark start dimming.

After all, that Errol Flynn look-alike you may have married 30 years ago by now may have a chest that has completed its slide into his stomach. And that shy little girl you took to the altar at the end of World War II may nag you so much by now that you're suggesting she join the Silent Majority (with emphasis on "Silent").

Anyway, I think it does us well occasionally to hear those young (or not-so-young) couples repeating their vows before God and everybody else. Promising things like "love, honor and cherish" and "in sickness and in health" and "till death do us part."

It appears the trend in weddings in recent years has been away from the promise of "love, honor and obey." That's a pity, too, because it used to be about the only thing that lent a little humor to the wedding ceremony.

I read the other day that marriage is on the upswing, and I'm glad to hear that. More couples are getting married in church ceremonies, it seems, although justices of the peace are busy performing weddings, too.

That reminds me of a man who once told me he'd been married by a justice of the peace. "But I think they ought to change their title," he said. "In 40 years of marriage, I haven't had either justice or peace."

Maybe he got stuck with one of those $3 marriage licenses.

(June 8, 1983)

10

Before Astroturf and aluminum bats

"Coach, can I go to the bathroom?"

Now, that's a question Billy Martin probably never had to contend with — not even once — in all the times he managed the New York Yankees.

But I must be asked that at least half a dozen times in my position as an assistant coach for Bozo's youth baseball team this season.

Well, actually, I'm more of an associate assistant than assistant, and the truth is I really don't do much coaching. Mostly I just try to get our 7- and 8-year-old pint-sized powerhitters lined up and ready to bat while answering questions such as, "But coach, where's left field?"

I'll have to admit it's sort of a strange feeling, watching Bozo playing the same position (second base) on the same ballfield where I played 25 years ago.

Funny, but Stewart Park looked a whole lot bigger to me when I was 8 years old.

The stands were bigger back then. Those old wooden bleachers, long since replaced by smaller aluminum stands, must have seated 500 people. There was a huge covered pressbox and a P.A. system, too.

"Randy Jones, third base," the announcer-scorekeeper would boom over the microphone, and Randy Jones would feel like a major leaguer when he stepped into the batter's box.

I remember they played the national anthem before every game, and every field had a flagpole (with a flag, yet!).

Hubert Gregg and his Seeing-Eye dog Buck were always there, making the trip from ballfield to ballfield, selling those peanuts. And midway through the game we'd stop long enough for somebody to pass a cigar box around the crowd for donations to help pay the light bill and other expenses.

We were the original Boys of Summer back then. It was back before Reggie Jackson and million-dollar contracts and before anybody I knew had even seen a soccer ball, much less played the game.

It was back before we had alleged major league baseball teams in Arlington and Houston. And it was back before aluminum bats.

It has long been my contention that God never intended baseball to be played with aluminum bats. There's something unnatural — no, make that un-American — about getting a hit and having the bat go "pinggg!" instead of "crackkk!" Baseball has just never been the same since the invention of the aluminum bat.

As youngsters growing up in our southside neighborhood, we lived and breathed baseball. It was the biggest thing in our lives. A kid who didn't collect baseball cards (five cards for a nickel, plus that hard pink gum that was impossible to chew) or who was afraid to play burnout in the backyard just didn't rate.

The kids in our neighborhood could tell you what Mudcat Grant's ERA was for the Indians, or how many homers Bill Skowron had hit for the Yankees, or how far Chicago's Nellie Fox could spit his tobacco juice.

Why, I even slept with my Louisville Slugger during the season (I mentioned this to Better Half several years ago and she was a little concerned until I explained a Louisville Slugger was a baseball bat. A wooden bat, naturally).

And I even remember checking out "20,000 Leagues Under the Sea" from the school library once because I thought it was a book about baseball.

It's only natural, I suppose, to imagine that as 7- and 8-year-olds we were turning double plays and making one-handed circus catches those many years ago. But the truth is, back in 1960 we also were asking the coaches where left field was.

And just like today, the coaches — the good ones — were stressing patience and sportsmanship and fundamentals, with emphasis on the fun.

But most importantly, they, too, knew where the bathroom was.

(May 29, 1985)

11

Jiminy! Those chirping crickets

I wound up sleeping on the couch the other night, and it was all because of him again.

"Him," I should explain, is a big black cricket.

The critter somehow found his way into our bedroom, where he began making a not-so-joyful noise loud enough to, well, to keep me awake. It was 2:31 a.m., too.

I can't be positive, but I believe this is the very same big black cricket that kept me from a good summer night's sleep a couple of years ago. The chirp sounds the same, only a little more mature. I never did find him that time and I figured he'd disappeared into our closet, never to be heard from again. Until Monday night.

Naturally, nobody else in the house was bothered by his a cappella singing. Only me. Funny, isn't it? I can fall asleep in a minute with the TV blaring, but an inch-long cricket grates on my nerves like chalk across a blackboard.

So there I was (it was 2:35 by now), lying with my head under the pillow trying to ignore the racket. It became apparent, however, that this would call for more than passive resistance. So I gingerly rose from the bed, grabbed a houseshoe and stumbled toward the sound in the pitch dark.

Now, my intention wasn't to kill the cricket. No sir. After all, I had grown up watching Jiminy Cricket on the Mickey Mouse Club show. To this day, crickets hold a place dear to my heart. It just wouldn't be cricket to kill a cricket.

Rather, the plan was to grab him up (I say him because I read somewhere it's the males who do all the chirping) in my shoe and to deposit him out the front door. But as I say, it was awfully dark and I wasn't sure where the racket was coming from.

I was sure, though, the cricket was probably smiling at me,

enjoying the thought of a grown man tripping over furniture at 2:37 a.m. trying to find him.

A couple of minutes later, I finally determined he was in the corner by the bathroom door. I could hear his little body thudding against the wall. By this time my patience was wearing a little thin (I think he was in the middle of a rendition of an old Buddy Holly tune). "Aggggggg!," I yelled, lunging toward him like something out of one of those karate movies.

Naturally I missed him, but succeeded in waking up Better Half. She was very sympathetic. "Go back to sleep," she said. Climbing back in bed, I rested my head on the pillow again. There was a lull in the cricket's serenade, but I knew it was only a matter of time.

Sure enough, a couple of minutes later (2:41 a.m.) he started up again. I also read somewhere that cricket sounds are affected by the temperature. It must be true because he was certainly making me hot under the collar.

Up again, shoe in hand, this time I decided Mickey Mouse Club or not, this cricket was going to buy the farm. "Come on," I said, doing my best Clint Eastwood impression, "make my night." But it was to no avail. The little critter again escaped my grasp, this time hopping behind the dresser. And no amount of coaxing would budge him.

Thoroughly defeated, I grabbed my pillow and staggered to the living room couch. "Got to get some sleep," I mumbled to Better Half, who didn't hear me because she was sound asleep again. I had just gotten prone when I heard an ominous hop, thud, hop coming down the hall.

The little critter was following me to the living room! Then he started chirping at a decibel only slightly higher than a Van Halen concert.

At 2:56, I made my way back to the bedroom and shut the door, leaving the cricket to his noise-making. He chirped off and on for the rest of the night. By morning, he was gone.

But he'll be back, I'm sure. He'll be back.

(August 8, 1984)

12

Stand up and be counted

Well, here it is April 1, Senator Harold Hoodwink, and I immediately thought of you.

No, senator, what I meant was today's National Census Day, the deadline to return those questionnaires to the U.S. Bureau.

Do you remember, senator, telling us how important it was to stand up and be counted? Well, now it's your turn.

That's right. As long as the federal government is sticking its nose into our business, we figured turnabout was fair play. So we taxpayers are taking our own census. We have a questionnaire for you.

Don't gripe, senator. After all, you're getting the short form. But remember — how you answer the form will determine whether you go back to Washington for another term.

Here are the questions:

1. Do you believe bureaucrat is a dirty word? (a) yes; (b) no.

2. Can you talk out of both sides of your mouth at the same time? (a) yes; (b) no.

3. Have you used any of these expressions within the past week? (a) "viable alternative;" (b) "budgetary shortfall;" (c) "revenue enhancement."

4. Do you like broccoli?

5. Do you believe there should be more openness in government? (a) yes; (b) no; (c) I refuse to answer.

6. When you hear the word dole, do you think of: (a) Robert? (b) Elizabeth? (c) pineapples? (d) big bucks?

7. How many zeroes in a trillion? (a) six; (b) nine; (c) 12; (d) does it really matter?

8. When someone speaks of Einstein's Theory of Relativity, do you associate that with getting more members of your family

on the government payroll?

9. Have you ever seen a political candidate talking to a rich person on television?

10. Who said, "The short memories of American voters is what keeps our politicians in office"? (a) Will Rogers; (b) Richard Nixon; (c) I don't remember.

11. Were you among the congressmen who voted themselves a fat salary increase? (a) yes; (b) no; (c) I don't remember.

12. For those congressmen who supported the salary increase, should they: (a) run for re-election? (b) run for cover?

13. To bring in additional government revenues, should Congress: (a) increase taxes? (b) increase user fees? (c) consider issuing gift certificates?

14. True or false: Do you think it's silly that a 78-year-old congressman can be referred to as a "junior senator"?

15. Which would you say we have more of: (a) congressmen who are trying to start an investigation? (b) congressmen who are trying to stop an investigation?

16. Which statement comes closer to the truth: (a) no drunken sailor ever spent money as fast as a sober congressman; (b) not only is Washington's face on our money, Washington's hands are on it, too; (c) I'd vote a straight ticket if I could ever find a straight ticket.

17. The biggest reason for waste in federal government is: (a) too much overhead; (b) too much underhand.

18. There is little danger of the federal government being overthrown because: (a) our military is too strong; (b) there's too much of it to overthrow.

19. Do you favor intelligence tests for government officials and/or those who would like to be? (a) yes; (b) no; (c) I don't understand the question. Could you repeat it?

20. Do you think Washington, D.C., qualifies as a disaster area? (a) yes; (b) no.

So there you have it, senator, and remember — if you don't fill out the questionnaire, we'll send someone to your house to make sure you do.

Happy Census Day, Harold. After all, what better time for the taxpayers to finally come to their senses?

(April 1, 1990)

13

Those nose-stuffing kids

Bright Eyes stuffed a Red Hot up her nose the other day. I say that rather matter-of-factly because I wasn't there when it happened. But Bright Eyes and her mother managed to get pretty excited about it.

I don't know what it is about three-year-olds and their noses (maybe they're just nosey at that age). But I do know it was four years ago when big brother Bozo, also three at the time, decided to stick a piece of soap up his own schnozolla.

Maybe it's a way for youngsters to thumb their collective noses at parental authority. But whatever the reason, it certainly got their parents' attention both times.

The latest incident started innocently enough. "Guess what I did, Mommy?" Bright Eyes said, walking into the kitchen holding a box of those little sugar-coated candies she'd received for Valentine's Day. "I put one up my nose." Better Half said she was smiling when she said it, too.

But it wasn't long before Bright Eyes quit grinning and her nose started burning. All of a sudden, stuffing a foreign object up the snout didn't seem like such a good idea after all.

Better Half's mind immediately flashed back to Memorial Day 1980, when Bozo had informed us about his own soap-up-the-right-nostril trick. At least then, he had a reason for doing what he did. "I wanted to see how it'd feel," he'd said. But Bright Eyes couldn't give us a specific reason for her own attempt at the world's record for Red Hot nose-stuffing.

Now, the first thing you realize in, er, tight situations such as these is that nothing really prepares you for them.

I mean, nowhere in Dr. Spock is there a section on removing

soap from the right nostril. You can't look in the yellow pages under "Red Hot Retrieval," either, and calling Roto-Rooter would probably be a bit too radical.

Better Half recalled that tweezers had proved ineffective in Bozo's case. So had my feeble attempts at humor. "He stuck soap up his nose?!" I'd said. "No lye?" She didn't think that was the least bit funny. Four years later, she still doesn't.

A box of Kleenex had turned the trick for Bozo in 1980, so she decided to try it with Bright Eyes this time. If a few well-aimed attempts at blowing out the Red Hot didn't work, then their last resort would be a trip to the doctor (Where we would surely wind up paying through the nose).

By this time, red stuff was slowly dripping out Bright Eyes' left nostril. Better Half thought it was blood at first, but fortunately it turned out to be the Red Dye No. 2 or whatever the heck it is they're putting into Red Hots nowadays.

A dozen blows and several tissues later, the little culprit finally emerged from her nose. And except for a slightly irritated nostril (Better Half was a little irritated, too, come to think of it), Bright Eyes is none the worst for wear.

Since relating this latest little adventure to some folks, I've heard tales about more three-year-olds who decided to use their noses to store everything from rocks and beans to raisins and peanuts. I'll spare you the details, however.

We don't expect to have any more problems with nose-stuffing efforts from Bright Eyes and Bozo. They've learned that doing something like that is a good way to ruin their noses (which I suppose you could say wouldn't make any scents).

And hopefully, this is the last time you'll see me writing a nasal passage such as this.

(February 17, 1984)

14

You, too, can be a Texan

OK, so you've just arrived from Ohio or Michigan or some other far-away land and you're suffering from an advanced case of culture shock in Texas, the land of high humidity and low humility.

Well, pardner, it's obvious you and other newcomers to Texas need a little help in understanding what the Lone Star State is all about. There are some things you need to learn pronto to survive in these parts, and the first is that just because you're living in Texas, doesn't necessarily make you a Texan. No siree.

But don't despair because I'm here to help. So listen up, follow my advice and you'll find yourself fittin' in faster than a New York minute. I suppose you could call this a Newcomer's Guide to Being a Texan. Read and memorize this list of do's and don'ts, and they'll be calling you "Tex" before long:

— We'll start off with the most important "Do" of all. If you're coming to Texas, do have a job.

— Don't start singing "I've Been Working on the Railroad" when somebody starts to play "The Eyes of Texas." You'll get a reputation as a party pooper. You may learn the official state song is actually "Texas, Our Texas," but don't bother about learning the words since most Texans don't know them either.

— Don't complain about Texans' lack of culture, and whatever you do, do not make such statements as, "We had a lot more things to do back in Toledo" or "That's not how it's done in Detroit." If things were so swell back in Toledo or Detroit, you'd still be there.

— Don't refer to the Gladewater Rodeo, or any Texas rodeo, as a "ro-DAY-o." You will get funny looks and people will ask you if you're from California.

— Always take off your hat in the presence of women or if

someone mentions Sam Rayburn (and for gosh sakes, don't ask anyone who Sam Rayburn is).

—If stopped by a member of the Houston Police Department, cooperate. Believe me, your life depends on it.

— Never — but never — suggest to a member of the Daughters of the Republic of Texas that Davy Crockett might have surrendered at the Alamo. Likewise, don't ever smile when you mention Santa Anna.

— Do not keep your out-of-state license plates six months after moving to Texas. Also, "I Love NY" bumperstickers are not recommended. Those should be replaced with something more appropriate, such as "America, Love It or Leave It," "Caution — Tobacco Chewer Ahead" or "Impeach William Wayne Justice."

—Do not tell Polish Jokes in Texas, but also do not tell Aggie Jokes in Texas. Native Texans can tell Aggie Jokes, and Aggies can tell Aggie Jokes, but the humor is lost when Aggie Jokes are told by someone from Atlantic City.

— Do not confuse the traditional Texas greeting of "Heidi" with the story of a little girl. The word means hello and you are expected to reply in kind.

—And that brings us to another important lesson in surviving in the land of urban sprawl and urban drawl. If you're going to live in Texas, you'll have to learn to speak the language. As you've no doubt noticed, Texans don't speak English. They speak Texan.

If expressions such as "tush hog" and "catty-wampus" and "peckerwood" and "gotch-eyed" have you scratching your head, you probably need to pick up one of several Texas vocabulary books available at most bookstores and libraries. Read a couple of 'em and pretty soon you'll be saying "Co-Cola" and "a lick and a promise" in no time.

— If you hear the expression "Tex-Mex," do not embarrass yourself by thinking they're talking about Lee Trevino. Actually, it's a type of Mexican food.

— Do realize that Texas remains the wide-open spaces, except when you're trying to find one at the mall.

—Learn the significance of March 2, April 21 and Juneteenth.

Well, that's a short course in Texas Culture, and it should be enough to let you pass as a Texan. And chances are most folks won't even ask where you came from.

That's because of a saying we've got in Texas: "Never ask someone where they're from. If they're from Texas, they'll tell you. And if they're not, you don't want to embarrass them." (June 9, 1982)

15

Making some orthodontist happy

In case you've been wondering, Bright Eyes doesn't have a growth in her mouth. That's only a thumb.

We've got friends who have never seen our year-old daughter without her thumb in her mouth. Sometimes it stays in there for days on end. It rarely comes out, and then only on special occasions such as mealtimes.

No doubt the thumb — it's the one on her right hand — will be permanently wrinkled and she'll have to go through life with a digit that looks like a prune (now isn't that the pits?). But while it may look bad, we've got to remember that some day she'll probably make an orthodontist very happy.

Big Brother Bozo had his "Bobby Blanket" for security as an infant, but Bright Eyes has her thumb. The thumb is a more practical choice. It's smaller, easily carried, and it goes everywhere she goes. No once has she misplaced her thumb.

Bright Eyes, thumb and all, celebrated her first birthday this week. And frankly, we were a little concerned that she would make it this far. Question: How do you drive a baby buggy? Answer: Give it an older brother.

You see, she's got a 4-year-old brother, and 4-year-old brothers can make it pretty tough on baby sisters. Still, she's a real trooper. During her first year she's survived the usual falls on the noggin' and even the log ride at Astroworld, so she's not about to let Bozo get the best of her.

This brown-eyed member of the college class of 2001 has honed her two weapons — biting and hair-pulling — during numerous confrontations with her brother. She's a world-class biter (no small feat considering she keeps that thumb in her mouth), and a tiny bald spot atop Bozo's head attests to her proficiency in hair-pulling. I mean, when she grabs hold, that blond hair comes out by the handful. Having a baby sister has been a real hair-raising experience for Bozo.

On the bright side, Bozo is also his sister's self-appointed protector, and the two of them usually get along well together. She also got through the first 12 months without any trips to the emergency room (Bozo had her beat 2-0 in that category). But she's a climber (she can climb anything), and it may be only a matter of time.

The past year has been one of discovery for all of us. Bright Eyes, for instance, has learned that chewing on the fireplace brick isn't a good idea.

The parents have learned they'd forgotten about all those dirty diapers and late night feedings and baby food all over the kitchen floor. We've also discovered that people automatically assume that all babies are boys. I never knew that before.

Admittedly, it's a little difficult at that age to tell the boys from the girls. But we can dress Bright Eyes in pink lace and stick a ribbon in her hair and invariably folks at the grocery store will still say, "Oh, isn't he cute?"

Thankfully, the hair's growing longer now. At the advanced age of one year, Bright Eyes is showing signs of growing tired of strained vegetables and other baby food. I suppose it won't be long before Bozo introduces her to such delights as pizza and that staple of all American youngsters, the venerable peanut butter and jelly sandwich.

But that thumb is still planted firmly in her mouth. I've decided it's hereditary. I was a thumb-sucker, too, and it evolved into an advanced stage in my adult life.

The only difference is that instead of a thumb in my mouth, nowadays, it's usually my foot.

(July 8, 1981)

16

'It's the Dalton Gang!'

Eighty-seven years ago this week, Longview was in mourning.

Its residents were burying popular George Buckingham and tending to the wounded, all victims of a May 23, 1894, bank robbery that even today stands as one of the biggest events in the city's history.

"The robbery of the First National Bank is the talk of the town," read one contemporary newspaper account. "If the robbers are taken alive there will be no expense to the state in the prosecution of them should they be brought back here. There is plenty of timber, plenty of matches and plenty of men willing to start a bonfire and anxious for a burnt offering to atone for the destruction wrought on Wednesday."

East Texans by the hundreds crowded Fredonia Street for days after the raging gun battle, counting the bullet holes in the walls and fences near the alley that is today known as Bank Street.

Here more than 250 shots were exchanged between the four bank robbers and the townspeople, and the toll was fearful. Buckingham had been gunned down by four slugs as he and J.W. McQueen emerged from a Tyler Street saloon to see what all the shooting was about.

Buckingham died in the alley but McQueen, "an old and well-known citizen and a Knight of Pythias," lived despite "a great hole clear through the abdomen from side to side."

Others were expected to die, too. City Marshal Matt Muckleroy suffered a serious pelvic wound after an outlaw's bullet glanced off a shirt pocket purse containing several coins. Charles Learned, a millhand, was hit in the leg as he walked through the courthouse yard behind the bank.

T.C. Summers was hit in the hand and bank cashier Tom Clemmons also sustained a hand wound when he struggled with one of the bandits.

One of the outlaws bit the dust, too. He was known locally as George Bennett, who worked at a sawmill and who recently had married a local girl. Several days after the robbery (which netted $2,001.58 in silver and small bills), Buckingham and the bandit were buried. It was a study in contrasts.

"At George Buckingham's funeral every store in town was closed and his remains followed by the largest crowd ever seen at a funeral here," an 1894 newspaper story told the readers. "Every face wore an expression of sadness and regret" as the body was carried from a little house on Fredonia Street to Greenwood Cemetery.

Outlaw Bennett (Bennett was an alias; his real name was Jim Wallace), however, was "carried to the grave in a city cart ... followed by no mourners, uncased in even a pine box, literally unwept, unhonored and unsung." He was buried in a potter's field, "as the carcass of a cow, removed as a stench in the nostrils of the community. The remains of Bennett, the robber, wait the final summons to appear at the place of readjustment, where all crooked things of the heart or body are made straight."

A few days later the shootout claimed a second Longviewite. Charles Learned had a leg amputated as a result of his wound, but he died May 31. Longview had another victim to bury.

A number of the city's residents couldn't attend the funerals. They were with Sheriff Jack Howard's posse, hot on the trail of the three remaining bandits. Only later did they learn they had been chasing one of the nation's most notorious desperadoes — the infamous Bill Dalton.

Dalton, whose brothers had been shot up in the famous Coffeyville, Kan., bank robbery attempt two years earlier, had masterminded the Longview bank job.

As it turned out, it would be some stolen bank notes from Longview that would eventually lead to Dalton's demise in early June 1894.

But then, that's another tale.

(May 27, 1981)

17

Note-writing bandit intimidated East Texas posse

On this very day in 1894, a posse of Longview horsemen was hot on the trail of three bank robbers.

But the capture was not to be. Of course, the bandits had a pretty good head start on the locals. And then again, it could have had something to do with the written death threat and two Winchester shells the bandits left waiting for the posse.

It was May 23, 1894, when four men held up the First National Bank of Longview. In the gunbattle that ensued, locals George Buckingham and Charles Learned had been killed and City Marshal Matt Muckleroy and Walter McQueen were gravely wounded. One gunman, identified as George Bennett, lay dead at Bank and Fredonia streets.

Sheriff Jackson Connor "Jack" Howard had quickly organized a posse of townsmen to go after the robbers.

Now, going after the robbers was one thing; but actually capturing them was another matter entirely.

Decades after the bank robbery, one of the posse members was interviewed by the News-Journal. The citizen, at the time of the robbery a youngster of 16, recalled that posse members had kidded Sheriff Howard about saying on occasion, "Let's go back, boys, we're getting too close."

Quite possibly, Howard's caution had something to do with the brashness of the desperadoes.

After the bank robbery, the bandits had hightailed it north out of town. Having a pretty good idea that a posse would be following, the outlaws paused in their retreat just long enough for their leader to give a note and two Winchester shells to a fellow they'd seen walking along the road. The man was instructed to deliver the note and shells to the posse when it came along, and he did as he was told.

The note read:

"You'll get plenty of these if you follow too close. (Signed) Charles Specklemeyer."

For several days and nights, the Longview posse pursued the outlaws but eventually lost their trail. It has been suggested that the written death threat put quite a damper on the Longview posse's enthusiasm to get too close to the robbers. Shortly after news of the robbery spread, however, posses were springing up all over East Texas. The Smith County sheriff picked some men "in pursuit of the Longview bank robbers...with a view to intercepting them," one paper reported.

In another newspaper account, this one from Daingerfield, it was reported that "a posse of men from Longview had the robbers surrounded at Avinger, a few miles east of here. Sheriff J.W. High of this place and a posse of officers from Pittsburg went down this evening on the train to help out the posse and if possible capture the robbers."

On May 25, the robbers were reported seen near Pittsburg, then at Cason, then near Mount Pleasant. There, Deputy U.S. Marshal Frank Foe, who said he thought he might know one of the robbers and therefore their destination, telegraphed that he was heading to Ardmore, in Oklahoma Territory, to head them off.

It was a prophetic move.

For the next two weeks, East Texas lawmen continued their search to no avail. It turned out the bandits had, indeed, crossed the Red River and entered Oklahoma. Then in early June, the lawmen got their first break when a $20 bank note — one that had been stolen from the Longview bank — turned up in Ardmore.

On the morning of June 8, 1894, a posse led by U.S. Deputy Marshal Loss Hart surrounded a farmhouse west of Ardmore and shot to death the outlaw leader, a short bearded man who'd drawn a gun on them. Inside the house was most of the money taken in the Longview robbery.

It turned out, of course, that the brash, note-writing leader of the gang was none other than Bill Dalton, at the time the best-known bandit in America. Only now, "Charles Specklemeyer" wasn't going to be writing any more notes.

(May 25, 1988)

18

Theft of bike hard for 9-year-old to understand

Bozo became a crime statistic this week.

Somebody came right up the driveway the other evening and took his new bicycle off our front porch.

Now, what happened to our 9-year-old certainly doesn't compare in importance with robberies and murders and other criminal acts we're always reading about. Bikes are stolen all the time. And, of course, Bozo's bike can be replaced.

But it's such a helpless feeling knowing something very dear has been taken from someone you love and there's not really anything you can do about it.

They didn't take our other bicycles, naturally. My red discount special and Better Half's black one — the one she won with Blue Horse coupons when she was 12 — were left untouched in the garage. And Bright Eye's tiny yellow bicycle, the one she hopes Santa will replace this Christmas, was still there too.

No, it was Bozo's new blue 10-speed, all-terrain bike that disappeared the other evening.

He was already in bed when we discovered it was missing, but he joined us while we went outside and searched and searched to no avail. And when it became apparent we weren't going to find it, the tears came as he stood in his pajamas at the edge of the driveway, looking one way and then another down the dark street.

"God isn't very happy about this," he said between sobs, trying to be brave about it. But after all, he was a 9-year-old who had just lost his bike.

What especially hurts is that he had earned the bicycle. He'd started saving his money more than a year ago, just for a new bike. During the summer he'd done yard work for us and for his grandparents. It was hot, dirty work, too. But finally he earned enough for a new bike.

We all went down to the store and watched him pick it out — a nifty 10-speed with straight handle bars and hand brakes. He handed the clerk the $115 he'd saved up and his eyes were beaming as he rolled the bike out of the store. Even his 6-year-old sister was proud of him.

That was a little more than a month ago.

We called the police department to report the theft, and a policeman came a few minutes later and asked questions and filled out a two-page report.

Why, it wasn't even dark outside when the bike must have been taken, we told him. And no, we hadn't copied down the serial number. After all, Bozo's always careful about his possessions. Besides, we told him, we live in a "nice" neighborhood.

The policeman was very professional, and very nice, and he seemed genuinely concerned about the theft. "I'm sorry about your bicycle, son," he said, patting Bozo on the shoulder, "but we'll do what we can to find it."

He said it was usually kids who steal the bikes, ride them a while and then dump them somewhere. "We recover a lot of bikes," he tried to reassure Bozo as he got back into his patrol car.

Bright Eyes was pretty upset the next morning. Not so much that her brother's bike was stolen, you understand, but that a policeman had been at our house and she'd slept through it.

I've always been of the opinion that far more youngsters would rather steal second base than a bicycle, and I still believe that. But nowadays we make sure we've locked the garage door at night and we keep an outside light on.

As I say, the bicycle can be replaced, and it will be if it doesn't turn up. But until then, Bozo waits and hopes.

Crime doesn't pay. But I know one 9-year-old who can tell you it sure does cost.

(September 17, 1986)

19

Campaigning for vice president

OK. I really didn't want to commit myself this soon, but it appears the timing is right.

I am pleased to announce to you, my fellow Americans, my intention to seek the office of vice president of these United States.

I've even come up with a catchy campaign motto. How does "Van For Veep" sound to you?

Not president, you understand. Vice president. John Glenn and Walter Mondale and at least a half-dozen more have already announced for president, so I figure I'd just be another pretty face in that crowded race. But nobody has announced for vice president yet, and I figure that makes me the early leader in the campaign for the second spot on the ticket.

In case you don't remember (and you probably don't), I made an unsuccessful run at the vice presidency back in 1980, too. Although I announced my candidacy early enough, in 1979, my grassroots support quickly turned to weeds and I wasn't elected.

But I'm serious about it this time, folks. I've learned a lot of political savvy with one campaign already under my belt. And besides, I turned 35 last month, meaning I could actually serve if elected.

My favorite comment on the office of vice president came from Thomas R. Marshall, who once said:

"Once there were two brothers. One ran away to sea, the other was elected vice president, and nothing was ever heard of either of them again."

Marshall, a two-term vice president under Woodrow Wilson (but of course you already knew that), apparently knew what he was talking about. If elected, I would join the likes of Charles W. Fairbanks, Daniel D. Tompkins, William R. King, Schuyler Colfax,

Richard M. Johnson and Garrett A. Hobart. They all served as vice president, were only a heartbeat away from the Oval Office, and consequently became only footnotes in American history.

Let's face it. The vice president just doesn't get any respect. Maybe it's because he doesn't do anything. On the surface it sounds like a swell job. But despite popular opinion (one that was held by the immortal Spiro Agnew), being vice president really doesn't mean you're the president in charge of vice.

The vice president has only two duties, really. One, he is presiding officer of the U.S. Senate. And two, he has to represent the president in out-of-the-way places like Swaziland and Gambia and Cleveland — generally, places where the natives throw rocks at your car or where the president simply has no interest in going.

Take George Bush (he's the present vice president, in case you'd forgotten). I was wondering what had happened to ol' George when I finally saw his picture in the paper the other day. He looked well and I was glad to know he was still alive and kicking.

John Adams, our first veep, probably summed it up well when he called the vice presidency "the most insignificant office that ever the invention of man contrived." See, I figure that's my kind of job. I can handle a position like that.

I'm already familiar with the way the federal government does business (having operated under a deficit spending program at home for several years). And although I have some definite opinions on the major issues of the day, as vice president I would be smart enough to keep them to myself since nobody'd be interested anyway.

So when the New Hampshire primary rolls around next year, remember "Van For Veep." And if you'll help me get elected in '84, my office will always be open. Feel free to call me anytime in Washington if you've got a problem.

I promise I'll be able to lay the blame somewhere.

(August 3, 1983)

20

Fit to be (neck)tied

"A tie is like kissing your sister." — Darrell K. Royal

A customer came up to me the other day and said, "You ought to write something about neckties." It turned out he doesn't like them either.

There is a misconception that when Darrell Royal, who coached the Texas Longhorns back when they could beat Oklahoma, uttered his famous line about ties, he was talking about football.

Nothing could be farther from the truth.

In fact, I have it from an occasionally reliable source that he actually was commenting on his disdain for neckties (Think now: When's the last time you saw Darrell Royal wearing a tie?).

Neckties and I have just never gotten along. Maybe it's because I have never figured out why we wear them in the first place. I mean, they just aren't practical like, well, hats.

There's nothing better that has been developed for baldness than hats. Beggars can pass hats around, and politicians can talk through them. Hats are practical. But about the only thing a tie is good for is covering up a missing button on your shirt.

I've had a love-hate relationship (I love to hate them) with ties ever since I was 8 years old. Back then I wore those clip-on ties, especially to church, and couldn't wait until I got a little bigger and could wear an honest-to-goodness tie tie.

Yes, it was the best of ties and the worst of ties.

Anyway, I grew up and, at 38, I find I now have a closet full of ties, some of which I haven't worn in years. In fact, there are some I haven't seen in years.

As a result, I find myself wearing the same three or four ties while all the others just collect dust. There is nothing that lasts as long as a necktie you don't like.

There are several problems with ties. First, they are either (a) too long, or (b) too short, depending on how good (or how poor) a job you did tying them.

Second, neckties keep changing. One year thin ties are in. But the next year, wide ones are in and thin ones are out. Then it's those scrawny little sawed-off-at-the-end ties that're in while the pointed ties are out. It's stripes one season, solids the next. I never can keep them straight.

Somewhere in Milan this fall, I'm sure there was a man holding a bolt of cloth who smiled to himself and said to a co-worker: "Well, Giorgio, we've sold 23 million thin ties this year. Let's announce tomorrow that WIDE is in for '87."

It's enough to make you fit to be tied.

Some tie wearers can cope with this better than others. I've got a friend, for instance, who doesn't mind his growing collection of ties. He tells me he's held on to some of his ties for so long, they've come back in style five or six times already.

Third, I already own six dozen ties and what do I keep getting for Christmas every year? Ties, naturally. But I'm not about to raise a big stink about it. I know a fellow who griped about the tie his wife gave him for Christmas one year. So the next year she gave him a sock.

Down through history, we've paid homage to the great inventors. There was Eli Whitney and the cotton gin, Alex Bell and the telephone, Whitcomb Judson and the zipper, even Harvey Kennedy and the shoelace.

But as yet, no one has stepped forward to take credit for inventing the tie. That's sort of a shame, too, because I and a lot of other men I know would dearly love to throw him a party.

A necktie party.

(October 31, 1986)

21

The Longview Race Riot of 1919

It was easily the saddest period in Longview's history. Little, if anything, is spoken now about what became known as the "Longview Race Riot." The events of July 1919 aren't something you'd like to brag about.

The trouble started in June that year when, the story goes, a black man made advances toward a white woman in Kilgore. The man was brought to Longview, the county seat, and a few days later died under mysterious circumstances.

In early July, The Chicago Defender, one of the leading black newspapers in the country, published an article about the man's death.

Angered by the story, a group of white men gathered at the home of a black school teacher whom they accused of submitting the article to the Defender. On a downtown street, they severely beat the teacher, and then the mood really turned ugly.

The night of July 11, 1919, a mob of whites gathered in downtown Longview while blacks began to gather in their part of town. Mayor G.A. Bodenheim and other level-headed civic leaders of both races asked the groups to disband. But Bodenheim and the others were ignored.

Along about midnight, the whites headed for the black teacher's house, ordering him to give himself up. Then a shot rang out — the whites blamed the blacks for firing the first shot, and the blacks blamed the whites — and the riot was on.

Men from both sides were armed, and pretty soon Longview sounded like a Civil War battle. Some accounts say more than 100 shots were fired. When the shooting ended some time later, several white men had been wounded.

The city's fire alarm was sounded and soon a large crowd of whites had assembled downtown. Rifles and ammunition were handed out, and at daybreak the mob again headed toward the black section of town. There the school teacher's house was torched, along with several other structures.

Enough was enough. Local officials phoned Texas Gov. William P. Hobby, who ordered a number of Texas Rangers to Longview as well as some 100 National Guard troops. They arrived July 12 and set up camp on the courthouse lawn.

Early July 13, trouble again flared when a black man and county officers exchanged gunfire. Later that day, the man was killed by "armed citizens," according to one newspaper account. At that point, martial law was declared and National Guard Brig. Gen. R.H. McDill ordered every firearm in Gregg County to be surrendered to him. Several thousand weapons were turned in, including those of the county sheriff and his deputies.

On July 14, arrests began, and eventually some 50 men, both black and white, were arrested for their involvement in the riot.

On July 15, a citizens' committee adopted a resolution "deploring and condemning the actions of the said negro ... in circulating the paper containing the scurrilous article" and also "condemning the actions of the white men and boys in setting fire to the houses ..."

Finally, on Friday, July 18, martial law was lifted and the militia and Rangers left. In an effort to promote better relations between the two races and to put the lawlessness behind them, none of the men arrested were ever tried for their participation in the riot.

Longview was not alone. The summer of 1919 was probably the worst period of racial tension in the nation's history. More than two dozen race riots occurred that summer, including Chicago, Knoxville and Washington, D.C.

(July 16, 1986)

22

Words can be downright troublesome

Words fascinate me. They always have. For me, browsing in a dictionary is like being turned loose in a bank. —Eddie Cantor

As a person who makes a living with words, I'm supposed to have a passable knowledge of the English language. But the truth is, there are plenty of words I tend to have trouble with. Take lectern, for instance.

Not only does the word lectern look funny when it's in print, but I never can remember what you do with it. I always have to get out the dictionary to determine that a speaker stands behind a lectern. That's different, of course, from a podium or a rostrum, which a speaker stands on, or a pulpit, which a preacher stands in.

Most of the time I can dance around the problem by using a synonym. A synonym, as you know, is the word you use whenever you can't spell the right word and therefore can't find it in the dictionary.

Etc. is another handy word to use when you can't think of the word you want. You see etc. used a lot in newspapers. So the next time you see etc., you'll know it was because a reporter or editor couldn't think of the right word.

Then there are words that can mean pretty much what you want 'em to mean. "Virus" is one. It's a Latin word used by physicians that means "Your guess is as good as mine."

Riffle is another troublemaker for me. The word means to leaf through a book or a bunch of papers, and isn't to be confused (but usually is) with rifle, which means to plunder or to steal.

Another is flounder, which happens to be a fish, but which also means to move about clumsily. Flounder also is typically confused with founder, which means to bog down or to become disabled.

Pompon is another word you generally won't find spelled correctly. Ninety-nine percent of the time, you'll see it spelled "pompom" in conjunction with cheerleaders. But the fact is, a pom-pom is a rapid-firing automatic weapon while a pompon is one of those crepe paper things cheerleaders throw around at the ballgame.

Politicking is another of those words that don't look right no matter how you spell them. And it's the same for picnicking, too. I really don't understand where the letter k came from (K mart, maybe?), but it's supposed to be there, according to Noah Webster.

I've all but given up on carat, caret and karat, too. Diamonds are weighed in carats, the proportion of pure gold used with an alloy is expressed in karats, and a caret is a proofreader's mark, I think. Sometimes I run into censer, censor and censure, too. I'd try to explain them but I'd probably be censured.

Using the wrong word can be pretty embarrassing sometimes. I remember reading a story a while back that described a "wench truck" in Dallas. I presume the writer was talking about a winch truck, but nowadays you never know. Especially in Dallas.

It can get awfully confusing. I'm told Satan is capitalized but devil is lowercase. It's spelled duffel, not duffle, and the Dr in Dr Pepper is spelled without a period. The proper spelling is dietitian, not dietician (another one I don't understand), and the correct synonym for earthquake is temblor, not tremblor.

There are plenty of others. Why, just in the "F" words you've got flack and flak, flier and flyer, flaunt and flout, flair and flare.

My word! It's confusing. No, in fact, it's worse than that.

As Samuel Goldwyn said, it is "in two words: Im possible."

(December 13, 1985)

23

Democrats heading for a convention record

I belong to no organized political party. I am a Democrat.
- Will Rogers, 1932

I love political conventions. I wouldn't want them to meet more often than every four years, of course, but I still love to watch them.

It's all pretty amazing when you consider how we choose the men — and finally, women — who'll seek the nation's highest offices.

Thousands of delegates show up for a few days, parade around in silly hats and pay as little attention as possible to what's going on at the podium. Then they fight tooth-and-toenail over other delegates' candidates, finally select somebody to the ticket and then go home preaching unity. It's amazing.

The Democratic National Convention meeting in the City by the Gay, er, Bay, is no different, although I must admit I was a little concerned at first.

On Monday night, the convention was actually 19 minutes old before one of the speakers mentioned Franklin Roosevelt. And it was 31 minutes after the opening gavel fell before JFK's name was brought up.

This namedropping is a little slower than in previous conventions, but the speakers quickly made up for it Monday and last night and proceeded to throw out the names of past Democratic chief executives every few minutes.

This is a tradition, of course, and naturally Will Rogers (where is he when we need him?) had an observation to make about the practice. Will said, "If you eliminate the names of Lincoln, Washington, Roosevelt, Jackson and Wilson, both parties' political conventions would get out three days earlier."

Another tradition the Democrats are upholding this week is use of the word "great." Everything is "great" at national conventions. San Francisco is a "great host city," we're told. Mario Cuomo made a "great keynote speech" Monday. The Mosconi Center is a "great hall" in which to conduct the party's business. And we had a "great rendition" of the Star Spangled Banner to kick off the day's activities.

Charles Manatt has been "a great party chairman" (even though Mondale thought he was so great he tried to dump him). And the convention's next speaker is always "that great senator" who, naturally, hails from "the great state of ..."

This year's Democratic convention is going for the record. During the first two sessions, I've counted 187 "greats," meaning they're only 63 shy of the record set at the 1976 Republican convention. Wouldn't it be, well, great if they broke the record?

Three other phrases that are dragged out and dusted off especially for national conventions are (1) "These United States," (2) "It is my great (there's that word again) honor and privilege" (honor and privilege always go together at political conventions); and, my favorite, (3) "Please clear the aisles."

I'm also looking forward to the roll calls tonight, because that's when the states and territories try to one-up each other with catchy little phrases. I suppose you can call it *statesmanship*.

Alabama will probably remind us it's the "home of Bear Bryant," which has absolutely nothing to do with electing a president but let 'em brag a little. Colorado will get a round of applause (and boos) as the "proud home of Gary Hart," and Guam will announce that's where "America's day begins."

Louisiana will note it's the home of this year's world's fair, and so it will go until they get all the way to the Virgin Islands which, I presume will make some comment about virginity.

Anyway, it'll be another entertaining show, and no doubt what Will Rogers wrote decades ago will still hold true:

"Ah! They was Democrats today, and we was proud of 'em. They fought, they fit, they split, and adjourned in a dandy wave of dissension. That's the old Democratic spirit. A whole day wasted and nothing done. I tell you, they are getting back to normal."

(July 18, 1984)

24

Thoughts on traveling by plane

It's amazing how small the world looks from 35,000 feet up. I have heard airline travel described as hours of boredom interrupted by moments of stark terror.

But infrequent air traveler that I am, I have never been bored on an airplane.

(To be honest, that's not quite true. I once was bored on a 22-hour flight from Seattle to Vietnam, when the flight attendants were all corporals and PFCs. I remember we all sang Army songs — none of which I can repeat here — to wile away the time. But that was a military flight and shouldn't count).

The truth is, I still get excited whenever I fly over the night-time lights of Wichita Falls. I suppose that says something about me, doesn't it?

I am still amazed, for example, that I can fly from San Francisco to Dallas in the same time it would take me to drive from Dallas to Longview. But then again, I am one of those people who still don't understand how a big airplane with 300 people and tons of luggage on board can get off the ground.

Having recently returned from California, however, I have decided to make some observations about air travel. For instance:

— Beware of signs that say "Remote Parking." What that means is, the airport is in Irving but the parking lot is in Denton.

— If you see someone named Jack on the plane or in the terminal, do not, under any circumstances, yell, "Hi, Jack!" That is considered bad form and could be hazardous to your health.

— Airports can be very lonely places, especially at night.

— No matter how early you arrive at the airport, you will have to stand in line and wait.

— Airplane travel is more expensive. The cost of going up is going up.

— It has been said you can't fool all of the people all of the time, but I've decided the airline schedules come pretty close.

— Do not refer to the flight attendant as a stewardess, especially if the flight attendant is a man.

—Generally there is not much to see in an airport terminal. I have been to Anchorage, but I can't tell you anything about it except that Anchorage was cold. I arrived at 2 a.m. and sat in the terminal. I didn't know any more about Anchorage than before I'd landed, but at least I can say I've been there.

I did see Colonel Sanders get off an airplane at Chicago's O'Hare Airport once, but that was an exception. As I say, generally there is not much to see in an airport terminal.

— Four engines are better than two, or one.

— No matter which side of the airplane you sit on, most of the sights will be on the other side. "If you look out your window, off to the left you will see the beautiful Great Salt Lake. Truly a sight to behold," the pilot will say. Invariably, I will be sitting on the right-hand side.

When I get home from a trip, people always ask if I flew over the Grand Canyon or the Mississippi River or some other natural wonder, and I always say yes. Not that I necessarily saw the Grand Canyon or the Mississippi River, you understand. Only that I flew over them.

— Airplanes fly so fast nowadays that it is possible to eat breakfast over Atlanta and get indigestion over Kansas City.

It was Will Rogers who, although an avid flier himself, cautioned against the need for such fast travel.

"I have never yet seen a man in such a big hurry," Will wrote, "that a horse or train wouldn't have got him there in plenty of time. In fact, nine-tenths of the people would be better off if they stayed where they are instead of going where they are going."

He probably has a point.

Then again, airplane travel does have its advantages. At least it lets you pass motorists at a safe distance.

(January 9, 1985)

25

Turning 'de-feet' into victory

His name was Earnest and he was from Chicago. And he wanted out of the Army.

That wasn't unusual that spring and summer of 1971. There were plenty of recruits at Fort Polk who wanted out of Uncle Sam's Army. But unlike the others, Earnest was determined to do something about it.

"My feet hurt," Earnest declared shortly after arriving at the post to begin basic training.

Earnest — a tall, lanky kid and a big White Sox fan from Chicago's South Side — was, like most of us, there compliments of the world's largest travel agency, the draft board. And more than likely he was going to wind up in Vietnam along with most of us. Except Earnest thought differently.

"My feet hurt," he repeated. "And besides, olive drab ain't my color."

Actually, Earnest didn't exactly fit in, with or without bad feet. Most everybody in my company was from Texas or Louisiana or Mississippi — Southern boys all — and then there was Earnest from the South Side of Chicago. He just seemed out of place.

It didn't take long — about a week after we'd started our training in the mosquito-infested swampland of Louisiana — for Earnest to put his plan into action.

"My feet hurt," he told the company commander, who gave him permission to visit the post hospital. Naturally, the doctor there didn't find anything wrong and sent him back to the company. But soon, all of the hospital staff at Fort Polk would get to know Earnest.

I suppose most every draftee at one time or another considered trying for an early discharge. Heck, I was on KP so often at Fort Polk that I thought about applying for a medical discharge because of dishpan hands.

Earnest and I were on KP together a couple of times, and I remember asking what he had been in civilian life. "Happy," he replied. And then he said, "My feet hurt."

Earnest began to limp everywhere he went. He limped in the chow line, limped on the rifle range, limped when he marched. He kept going back to the post hospital. "My feet hurt," he repeated, and after a while a couple of the doctors decided there might be a problem here after all.

It could be fallen arches, said one. Flat feet, said the other. So instead of marching out to bivouac or to the firing range, they decided it would be better for Earnest to ride to the locations. They also told Earnest to stay off his feet. So it wasn't uncommon to find Earnest in the barracks, lying on a bed with his feet elevated on a couple of pillows.

It appeared Earnest was getting a leg up on the U.S. Army.

Now, not everybody was trying to get out of the Army. There was Red, a country boy from Deep East Texas who would have put Rambo to shame. Red loved basic training. He could shoot straighter, run faster and throw a grenade farther than anybody at Fort Polk. So naturally, when we finished basic and received our assignments, Red was made a clerk-typist.

To the other extreme was Waldo, who was from Houston and was, I'm sorry to say, a total klutz. Once while the company was out marching, Waldo misplaced his rifle. Just flat set down his M-16 and couldn't find it. Waldo graduated from basic, was sent to the tank corps and I believe eventually was assigned to the Pentagon.

Like most of the trainees, I wound up in Vietnam. And Earnest?

The sixth week of training, a bus pulled up outside our barracks. I remember Earnest was waiting there in his civilian clothes, taking shots at the goal on the company basketball court. I watched him as, several times, he leaped high and executed a perfect slam dunk. Then he picked up his bags, grinned real big and boarded the bus for the trip that would take him back to Chicago's South Side. Suddenly, Earnest was feeling no pain.

It had been quite a feet — er, feat.

(June 1, 1988)

26

That East Texas weather

"Looks like it's startin' to clabber up," said the gentleman, looking out a window at the darkening East Texas sky.

Now, that might sound a little funny to some folks. And if you're from Sandusky or Altoona or somewhere like that, it might have you running to Webster's to see what "clabber up" means. But I doubt you'd find it in there anywhere.

Weather has always played a big role in East Texans' conversations, ranking right up there with religion, politics and football (but not necessarily in that order). And because of its importance, down through the years East Texans have developed their own unique weather vocabulary.

When locals are discussing the weather, especially old-timers, you won't hear them talking about scattered thundershowers or high pressure cells or any of those other meteorological terms you hear on the 10 o'clock Big City weathercast. No sir.

Take Monday's rain. Now, that might have been just a locally heavy thunderstorm to the National Weather Service, but to lots of East Texans it was "a stump-mover" or a "chunk-floater" or a "gullywasher." As the gentleman at the window told me, "Looks like we're gonna be in for a real fence-lifter." And he was right.

Sure enough, the sky did clabber up, a thunderstorm bigger'n Dallas rolled in, and we had ourselves an honest-to-goodness root-searcher. I mean, it rained cats and dogs.

A couple of years ago after an especially hard rain, I heard a long-time resident say we'd had a "sure-nuff goose drowner." And one of my kinfolk up in Red River County told me once that they'd had a "clear-up shower." That meant it'd come down so hard it'd rained clear up to the front porch.

Just once, I'd like to hear the TV weatherperson quit talking about a "60 percent chance of rain" and a "stationary front over the Trans-Pecos Region" (I'm not even sure where the Trans-Pecos Region is located; after all, it hasn't come up in any of my conversations since I had sixth-grade geography) and say something like:

"It's clouding up, folks, and it looks like it's going to rain knuckles and bullfrogs." Or: "It'll be cold enough tonight to freeze the horns off a brass billy goat." Or even: "Get your ducks in a row because we've got a storm bigger'n a number three washtub brewing in the west."

See, I think TV weather ought to be a lot simpler than it is. Folks don't tune in to hear about wind-chill factors and how far the "mercury" is going to drop because they can't relate to that. It really doesn't mean anything to them.

But if you tell East Texans it's going to be hog-killing weather or that it's liable to "rain hub deep to a wagon wheel," then they know what you're talking about and they'll know they need their heavy coats and umbrellas.

Instead of pollution indexes and pollen counts and upper-level troughs, we need to know if it's "fairing off" or if it'll be colder than a well-digger's, er, backside, or if we're going to have a red sunset (because, as any East Texan knows, a red sunset usually precedes rain). I wonder if TV weatherpersons know that, or that if it thunders before seven it'll rain before 11?

I'm afraid it'll probably be a cold day in August before we start hearing forecasts like that. But one of these days, though, maybe the TV weather will get a little more down-to-earth with more of an East Texas accent.

Of course, that's only if the Lord's willing and the creeks don't rise.

(February 2, 1983)

27

Hubert Gregg, the Peanut Man

Just in case you didn't know, today is a red-letter day in our history. No, I don't mean San Jacinto Day, but rather something more important.

For you see, it was exactly 50 years ago today that Hubert Gregg started selling peanuts in Longview.

"Yep, it was April 21, 1932," recalled Gregg, the blind vendor who is known by most people as simply the Peanut Man. Down through the years, Gregg has become one of the city's best known and most respected residents.

Gregg came to Longview in 1931 from El Dorado, Ark. First he sold silver and glassware polish, and later newspapers in front of the old Hollywood Cafe. But the following year he heard about a minor league baseball game that would be played here. "It was Shreveport and San Antonio, and I went to the promoter — I think his name was Numpson or something like that — and asked him if I could sell peanuts at the game," Gregg said. "Well, he said yes, and I decided that night I'd make my living doing that."

And that's what he's been doing ever since. He has a downtown route, which is two to four days a week depending on whether he can get a ride downtown, and pulls the familiar red wagon behind him hawking the goobers. He's also sold peanuts at Longview Lobo football games since 1945 ("I haven't missed too many of the games over the years") and has been making the rounds at youth baseball parks since 1951.

It was at the ballparks where I first got to know Gregg (That's what all the kids called him, by the way. Just "Gregg"). I was eight years old and all of us pee-wee athletes would crowd around Gregg and pet that big guide dog he had. The boxer was named Buck and he was a beautiful animal and the best natured dog I've ever seen. He loved children and children loved him.

"He was some dog," Gregg said. "I loved him better than any

of the other dogs I had."

Gregg is one of those folks who never age. He doesn't look a day older today than he did 25 years ago. Maybe it's because he stays busy. "Oh, I get lazy sometimes. But all of us do," he grinned. "But the important thing is not to get in a hurry because that'll give you ulcers."

Gregg's wife of 20 years, Lina, died two years ago. But he's got four stepchildren, two who live in Dallas, and enough other interests to keep him plenty busy. In fact, right now at the age of 83, Gregg's taking cooking lessons.

He's come a long way since his childhood in Nebraska, when meningitis cost him his sight at the age of six. As a young man he tuned pianos and organs and played at revival meetings in the Midwest. He operated a tobacco stand in Arkansas for a decade, but then El Dorado's loss was Longview's gain.

Millions of roasted peanuts later, Gregg says he has "no regrets. I've had my ups and downs, but I get to get out and meet people. And they've been darn good to me. Longview's been good to me."

Fifty years later, Gregg shows no signs of slowing down. Today you'll find him selling goobers at the Chamber's General Business and Service Exposition out at the Gregg County Fairgrounds, and he's already made plans for the upcoming youth baseball season. "It starts May 17, you know," he said.

It has long been my contention that not enough people get monuments. So the next time somebody wants to name a ballfield or a park or something like that after somebody, may I submit Hubert Gregg's name? I can't think of anybody more deserving of the honor.

But until that happens, I suppose a simple "happy anniversary" will have to suffice.

(April 21, 1982)

28

Picking a color isn't that easy

It seemed a simple enough task.

We were going to paint Bright Eyes' room, see, and Better Half sent me down to the paint store to buy some yellow paint. And that's what I asked for.

"I'd like some yellow paint, please," I told the friendly paint store man.

"I'm sorry, sir," replied the paint store man matter-of-factly as he placed a can of paint thinner on the shelf, "but we don't carry yellow paint."

I stood there a moment, pondering the meaning of that statement. "What do you mean you don't carry yellow paint? This is the paint store, isn't it?" I asked, glancing nervously for the big store sign out front. After all, with my sense of direction, I could have wandered into a sporting goods store.

"I mean, sir, we don't have a standard 'yellow' paint," the paint store man said. "We carry various shades of yellow. Now then, which shade of yellow did you want?"

"Well, let's see," I said. "Just put the cans on the counter and I'll see what I like," figuring he'd have five, maybe six shades of yellow to pick from. Wrong.

"I'm afraid that's quite impossible," he said, reaching toward a display that featured what turned out to be scores — no, hundreds — of tiny colored strips. "But we do have a number of samples to choose from. Here, which one do you like?"

This was beginning to become a bit more complicated than I'd bargained for. Heck, I didn't even want to paint Bright Eyes' room anyway. I mean, so what if it still had the original paint job from 10 years ago? Or was it 15? The paint was holding up well. At least, in spots it was.

"How about Shadow Yellow?" the friendly paint store man

asked. "It's popular this year. Or maybe this one. Lemon Fizz."

Lemon Fizz? He continued. "Then there is Lichen Yellow, Olive Yellow, Lemon Freeze, Gumdrop Yellow, Pansy Yellow, Yellow Primrose, Buttercup Yellow, Dandelion Yellow, Squash Blossom, Yellow Lily, Chiffon Yellow, Pineapple Yellow, Yellow Lime, Peace Yellow, Mimosa Yellow, Moonlite Yellow—just stop me when you see one you like — Nymph Yellow, Panama Yellow ..." When he got to Panama Yellow, well, that was the last straw.

"Blue," I blurted out.

"Excuse me?" the paint store man said.

"I, er, blue. I've decided I'd rather have blue," I said. Surely, I figured, there wouldn't be that many blues to choose from. There's blue, dark blue and light blue, right? I also knew Better Half would probably kill me. But there was no way I could choose from all those yellows. Surely she'd understand why we had to do our 4-year-old daughter's room in blue. Surely.

"Of course, sir," said the paint store man, again reaching for the display. "We have this nice Sailor Blue, not to be confused with Navy Blue or Marine Blue. And here's Tropic Blue, Ripple Blue, Anglin Blue, Reservoir Blue, Aqueduct Blue, Dutch Blue, Cloud Blue, Airy Blue, Dew Drop Blue, Satin Blue, Winter Blue, Halo Blue, Cape Cod Blue, Windmill Blue, Plymouth Blue, Gossamer Blue, Downy Blue, Cruise Blue, Demure Blue ..." By this point I was considering some off-color remarks of my own, but I couldn't. The paint store man was being so nice about it.

"I've changed my mind again," I said, changing my mind again. Just give me a couple of buckets of white paint. That's white, as in W-H-I-T-E, OK? Here, how much do I owe you?"

But, of course, it wasn't that simple.

"We have a fine selection of white," the paint store man said. "Would you prefer a nice Alabaster White, or possibly a Scallop White? And then there's Cameo White, Lighthouse White, Albino White, Heather White, Downy White, Dove White, Stormy White, Bon Bon White, Mummy White, Nordic White ..."

It was all too much. I left without buying any paint. Better Half had to come back to the paint store and purchase it. It's some shade of yellow, and it's pretty, but I don't know what they call it. But I do understand now why it's said old painters never die. They just kick the bucket.

Or could it be that they've gone stir crazy?

(June 26, 1985)

29

Christmas will miss him

It was a coincidence, I suppose, but the first day I noticed Christmas decorations in the store was the day David Romero died.

For almost two decades, the Hallsville resident had given East Texans a very special Christmas present. It was called Romero's Christmas Spectacular, and every December thousands of visitors trekked to his home to view a fantasyland of lights.

Over the years, a trip to Romero's became a tradition for our family and many others. Why, it just wasn't Christmas season until we'd been to Hallsville.

The Spectacular was, well, unlike anything you've ever seen before. There, covering an acre or so, were what seemed like thousands of strands of multicolored lights hanging from the trees.

Just inside the entrance way was a life-sized Nativity scene, and the brick paths that wound through the beautifully landscaped gardens revealed other delights. There was a Santa's workshop and a country store, wishing wells and religious shrines, a doll playhouse and the sweet gum tree Mr. Romero decorated with old jewelry and other items most folks would have thrown away.

There was always something new at Romero's. During the year, he would collect the lights and display items from garage sales, Goodwill stores, the dump, wherever. He would lovingly, painstakingly create holiday scenes. And come December, he would open his house to the world.

"I do it for the kids," he told me one year as he stood back, arms folded, looking very pleased as wide-eyed youngsters peered into Santa's workshop to view Mr. Claus' toy shop and a roaring fireplace. "I think they enjoy it the most."

He had suffered a stroke in August, but even from the nursing home bed he continued his plans for a Christmas Spectacular 1988. Friends promised him they would do the construction and continue the Romero's tradition if, for some reason, he was unable to.

Some Christmas memories stand out, of course. There is Romero's, and another that is very special to me is Christmas Eve of 1971. It was on that particular night that I was on guard duty at Long Binh, Vietnam, staring into the darkness past the concertina wire and claymore mines that surrounded our bunker.

The other GI and I in the bunker that night talked about Christmases past and how this one was so different from the rest. And while it was Christmas, we were certain this was going to be just another boring night of guard duty.

But shortly before midnight, the stillness of the night was ended when, on the far side of the enormous U.S. Army base, someone began firing his M-60 machine gun. For a moment we held our breath, fearing that it must be a Viet Cong attack. But turning toward the firing, we could see the tracer bullets flying straight up into the air.

And then it dawned on us. There was no attack. It was just a bored soldier stuck on guard duty on Christmas Eve, and he was trying to celebrate Christmas the only way he could. Moments later a second bunker began firing, then a third and a fourth. It wasn't long before dozens of bunkers, including ours, joined in.

For a few minutes, the midnight sky over Long Binh was brightly lit by hundreds of tracer bullets. It was a beautiful sight, and I couldn't help wondering if the sky over Bethlehem had been that bright 2,000 years earlier.

And you see, in his own way Mr. Romero helped make Christmas brighter — much brighter — for East Texans every year.

There were a couple of times that I wanted to call him up to thank him for what he did, and then I got busy and, regretfully, never got around to doing it.

But somehow, if friends really do come through and continue the Hallsville tradition, I suspect that will be all the thanks David Romero would want.

(Oct. 16, 1988)

30

Saddled with the job of columnist

I knew it would happen sooner or later.

My column's due, and I'm sitting at my trusty terminal without the slightest idea of what I should write about today. After more than five years and nearly 600 columns, my mind is a total blank (Better Half would respond, "So, what's new?").

But instead of looking for the panic button on the keyboard, this appears to be a really good opportunity to discuss what it's like to be a columnist.

I get a lot of questions from folks who want to know the ins and outs of column-writing. So here's a little insight.

The most-often asked question is, "How did you get to be a columnist?" (Usually the person asking the question puts great emphasis on the word "you").

Answer: First, you have to be able to type. Second, nobody else wanted to do it.

The second most-often asked question is, "How much do you get paid to be a columnist?"

Answer: That's a tacky question and you ought to be ashamed for asking it. I'm a nosey journalist and I can get away with asking a question like that, but you're the public and you can't. Besides, if I told you my salary, you'd be as embarrassed about it as I am.

The third most-often asked question is, "How far ahead do you write your columns?"

Answer: Usually, about 10 minutes before deadline. I read about a columnist once who was so prolific that he stayed weeks ahead of deadline. In fact, I'm told he'd write up a storm and always have about 200 columns already written and ready to run in the paper. Of course, he's also dead now, too, and I figure that's probably what killed him.

At some newspapers, the columnists have it rough because

all they do is write columns. The rest of the time they just sit around, dreaming up column ideas and twiddling their thumbs. How awful! Fortunately, it's not like that here. My bosses are kind enough to let me cover City Hall and a dozen other activities, too.

There are a few other basic tips for writing a regular column. Naturally, you must have a reasonable command of the king's English. Don't use no double negatives. Make each pronoun agree with their antecedents. Make sertain you're speling is korect. Things like that.

Writing a column also makes you an expert in the eyes of some people, possibly because columnists are always giving out such gems of wisdom as, "Never buy a television set on the sidewalk from a man who's out of breath."

Columnists also are fond of using big words such as lucubration and sententious or peripatetic. But you'd better know the meanings of any words you use because the readers will sure call you up and ask you what they mean.

Because they see your picture in the paper, strangers aren't the least bit shy about calling you up late at night — usually during your favorite TV program — to offer suggestions. "Say," they'll say, "why don't you write a lighthearted column about advanced techniques of brain surgery? I bet you could get something real funny out of that!"

They also figure you must be an expert on everything since you write a column. That's why people write or call to ask strange questions like who carried Upshur County in the 1956 Democratic senatorial primary or what day of the week was it on May 18, 1742.

Of course, having your picture on a column also can be a liability since it could get you a fat lip from somebody who took offense about something you wrote.

That's why a columnist always needs to remember that the power of the printed word is strong indeed ("Freedom of the press," I read once, "is confined to those who own one"). It's awfully easy to hurt people.

But while being a columnist can be a real ego trip, I and others of my ilk would do well to remember the words of Will Rogers:

"The funnies occupy four pages of the paper, and editorials two columns. That proves that merit will tell."

Ouch.

(April 11, 1984)

31

Money's only good to owe nowadays

I've decided about all you can do with money nowadays is owe it.

It'd be a lot easier, of course, if the neighbors would just quit buying things you can't afford.

You know what I mean. The family down the street buys a new gadget, and pretty soon you're the only one on the block without one. Keeping up with the Joneses is a full-time job.

The best things in life might be free, but unfortunately the essentials cost money. And the list of "essentials" is constantly expanding. Ice boxes used to be just fine, and then along came refrigerators. Ceiling fans did the trick, too, until air conditioning was invented. And that was fine, because refrigerators and air conditioning were big improvements.

But then it started getting out of hand. Pretty soon, one radio wasn't enough. We needed two or three, or maybe one in every room. Then it was the same for telephones and television sets. Now we've got phones and TVs all over the house, because they've become "essentials" too.

From there the list expanded (exploded might be a better word), and now we wonder how we ever got along without that blender, microwave oven, home computer, automatic garage-door opener, swimming pool, tennis court or third (or fourth) car. They've all become, well, essential.

As a result, some people are going to have trouble deciding which car to drive to the poorhouse. Too many Rolls-Royce tastes and sub-compact incomes, you might say.

People are funny. They spend money they don't have to buy things they don't need to impress people they don't even care for. Then they scratch their heads and wonder how they ever got in such a mess.

But it's clear to me that most folks' financial problems are quite simple: They're short of money.

Americans tend to operate under what I call the Out-go Exceeds the Income Principle, similar to the system Uncle Sam has used so successfully for so many years (If George Washington never told a lie, then what's his picture doing on a $1 bill that's only worth about 37 cents?).

Time was, it was true what Ben Franklin said: "A penny saved is a penny earned." But that was, of course, before the sales tax was invented.

It bothers me whenever I hear somebody refer to money as "dough." That's a misnomer since dough sticks to your hands. It's true money talks, but mostly it just says "goodbye."

The poor gripe about the money they can't get, and the rich complain about the money they can't keep.

Some people spend money because they believe the axiom that "You can't take it with you" when you die. But taking the money with you when you die isn't the problem. The problem is making it last until you're ready to go.

A few Americans are trying to save up money with the hope it'll be worth something one of these days. Some are supporting their churches through tithes. Although you can't take it with you, they figure they can at least send it on ahead.

But it's getting harder and harder to save money nowadays. Some time back, a fellow told me a "balanced budget" was defined as being when the month and the money run out together. That was the nice thing about February. It only had 28 days.

Maybe all we need to solve our money problems are shorter months.

(March 1, 1985)

32

A humbled Dizzy Dean

It was the night Ol' Diz wowed 'em in Longview, and learned a little humility in the process.

Jay Hanna "Dizzy" Dean was one of baseball's most colorful figures, whether tossing strikes from the mound or throwing out his own particular brand of the king's English from the broadcast booth.

He also wasn't exactly shy when it came to bragging about his pitching abilities or those of his brother, fellow St. Louis Cardinal teammate Paul "Daffy" Dean.

In 1934, Dizzy and Daffy won 49 games for the Cardinals, and Dizzy won another 28 the following season.

Now it was October 1935, and the folks in Longview were pretty excited — although a little skeptical — about a post-season pitching exhibition 24-year-old Dizzy was scheduled to put on at the old Fair Park field on the south end of town. You see, there seemed to be some doubt that Ol' Diz would follow through on his appearance.

A couple of days earlier, Dizzy had refused to take the field in Chattanooga when he saw that only 300 paying customers had shown up. Learning his exhibition pay would be a meager $40, he told the Tennessee officials, "I wouldn't even walk out on the field for forty dollars." With that, he packed up and headed for New Orleans, where he also left promoters there holding the bag because of another small turnout.

In Longview, however, the locals were more than thrilled to have major leaguers trek through their part of the East Texas piney woods. Why, just Oct. 5, a huge crowd had showed up to see the great Rogers Hornsby himself — to this day still regarded as the greatest right-handed hitter of all time — lead a group of American League all stars in a local game against a semi-pro outfit.

But now the citizenry was speculating on whether Dizzy would take the mound in Longview, judging from his temper tantrums in Chattanooga and New Orleans.

On Saturday, Oct. 19, 1935, Dizzy arrived in Longview for his pitching duties with a game featuring two oil company semi-pro teams. By game time that night more than 1,500 jammed into the park to see the young Arkansas native who had been setting the National League afire. They weren't disappointed.

Dizzy "stepped upon the mound at Fair Park Saturday night and hurled a brand of ball seldom seen in this section," reported the Longview Daily News. "He pitched as beautiful a brand of ball as the customers could ask for, and gave them the show they came to see."

In his outing, the paper reported "the bragging, boasting Dean struck out seven batters, collected himself a hit, stole three bases and made one sacrifice." But the biggest hit, of course, had been Dizzy, and he was most appreciative of the fans' reception. He realized just how badly people wanted to see him pitch, and just how mistaken he'd been in walking out of the earlier exhibitions. So following the Longview game, he decided to right the wrongs in Chattanooga and New Orleans.

He headed down to the Western Union office and dispatched telegrams to the wronged promoters. "Realize I made mistake by refusing to play game," the telegram read. "If you will forward to me amount of loss in promoting game, I will pay it," Diz said, even offering to put on pitching exhibitions for free.

It probably was one of the few times in Dizzy's life that he had been humbled.

An injury cut short Dizzy's career in 1941, but it wasn't enough to keep him out of the Baseball Hall of Fame. Later he went into broadcasting, where he became famous (infamous?) for his declarations that players had "slud into second" or had "throwed a curveball" that broke so much it had "come by way of Port Arthur."

Dizzy Dean, the second-grade dropout who possibly was the most colorful personality major league baseball ever knew, died July 17, 1974.

(August 5, 1987)

33

Those dreaded essential elements

"All of us learn to write in the second grade, but most of us go on to greater things." — Bobby Knight, Indiana basketball coach.

Boy, I can't wait for school to start," Bozo said, stuffing his backpack with pencils and paper and placing it next to his brand new Scooby Doo lunch kit.

Tomorrow morning would be the start of another school year, and our 7-year-old was starting the second grade.

"Well, sit down here beside me," I said, patting the couch, "because I've got something here I'm supposed to read to you." The note from school officials said I was to read Bozo a small booklet outlining what was expected of him from his school, H. Ross Perot and the 67th Texas Legislature.

The Legislature, in its infamous wisdom, has decided to overhaul the state's public school system. Elected officials got the idea after realizing that the trouble with school dropouts wasn't that they couldn't see the handwriting on the wall, but rather that they couldn't read it.

"This little book will tell you what to expect this school year," I told Bozo. "It'll help you avoid any pre-school jitters. I suppose you're a little nervous about the first day of school. Right?"

"Nah, Dad. I'm excited," Bozo replied.

"Well, anyway, it says here I'm to point out your essential elements and descriptors for the school year," I said.

"What does that mean?" Bozo asked, writing his name on a notebook.

"Now, don't interrupt me," I said. "I'm explaining something to you. It says here in the booklet that you'll have two hours and 30 minutes daily of English language arts. Take reading, for instance. This year you'll learn word attack skills, use complex phonics such as initial blends, digraphs and diphthongs; use complex structural analysis such as root words and common affixes and, of course, use context clues."

Bozo just looked at me, a confused look on his face. "What does that mean, Dad? Aren't we going to read this year?"

I had to admit I was a little confused, too. I turned back to the booklet's cover just to make sure I had the right one. "Essential Elements: Grade Two," it said.

"Er, let's see what it says about arithmetic," I said, skipping over to Page 7. I began reading:

"Mathematics include the following essential elements (there were those words again): Understanding of numbers — whole, integer and non-negative rational, and place value system. The student will acquire number concepts through comparing, ordering, skip counting and investigating odds and evens."

"Huh?" asked Bozo. "You mean we aren't going to do any adding or subtracting?" I noticed he'd begun to fidget.

To be honest, after reading from the booklet, I wasn't exactly sure just what the heck it was saying. I quickly thumbed to the section marked "Science." It said second graders will have a science course with "a balance of content and activities" featuring such "Manipulative laboratory skills as using scales and balances, thermometers, using comparators such as mass, volume, symmetry, temperature, texture, size, shape and ..."

I stopped in mid-sentence when I noticed Bozo starting to get up. "Where you going?" I inquired. "You told me second grade was gonna be fun," he said. "But I don't understand any of that. I'm not going to school. I'm gonna stay in my room until I'm 18."

As he ran down the hall, I called out, "But here's Physical Education! You'll like PE. It says you shall be provided opportunities to participate in developmental activities related to muscular strength and endurance, flexibility and cardiorespiratory endurance, not to mention locomotor and nonlocomotor skills."

Texas schools have come a long way since I graduated back in 1966 B.C. (Before Computers). Youngsters who used to clean erasers now dust terminals. From log school to log on, so to speak. And I'll have to admit Better Half and I are ready for school to start, even if Bozo isn't.

After all, school days can be the happiest days of your life. Especially if your kids are old enough to attend.

(August 17, 1984)

34

Nobody can fill Papaw's shoes

Daddy, I'm going to miss Papaw," Bozo said, looking at the blue casket.

For the first time in his young life he was coming face to face with the reality of death, and he had a lot of questions. But he understood that he wouldn't be seeing his grandfather anymore.

My father-in-law had been sick ever since Bozo had been born six years ago. But during all that time, even with all the treatments and the trips back and forth to Houston, I never heard him complain. Not once. But then, that's the way he was.

He was a man of few words. Mostly he just let his actions speak for him. He was always doing something for somebody. At the funeral home almost everyone had a tale to tell about his generosity. About lumber he had given to help a neighbor build a house. About food he had given another family years earlier when times were hard and winter was coming on. About money he had given to help a friend out.

And he never expected anything in return. Why, even thanking him for a kindness rendered seemed to embarrass him. Some people are givers and others are takers. He was a giver.

He was one of those people who could fix or make anything, from repairing the engine in the old green pickup to making wooden candleholders to sell at the church Christmas bazaar. He had a workshop in the garage and that's where you could generally find him — turning pieces of wood into things of beauty — until the illness just wore him down and it got to be too much of an effort.

And you would have never guessed this big, burly man would take an interest in painting something like birds, but he did. He'd cut out the blocks of wood and with delicate strokes paint redbirds and bluebirds on them. He enjoyed that, and he was good at it, too.

He had a devoted wife who loved him very much, and he loved her, too. And two children that he was so proud of.

And then there were the grandchildren. There were four of them and they were the joy of his life. His eyes would sparkle when one of them would climb up into his lap, and whenever he'd put on that old baseball cap and head out to tend to the garden there'd be four little shadows tagging along right behind him. And a trip to Papaw's generally meant a ride on the tractor.

Actually, it was a riding lawnmower with a small trailer hooked behind it. But the grandchildren called it a tractor, and he was never too busy to take them for a ride. There were times, of course, that we knew he was hurting, but he'd never let on. The grandkids wanted to ride the tractor, and that's all there was to it.

So they'd all pile into the back, grinning from ear to ear and hanging on for dear life, and for the next 20 minutes or so he'd take them bouncing over hill and dale and around the "booger house." That's what they called the dark, deserted house next door.

But Papaw's tractor rides have ended now. The illness finally got the best of him, as we knew it eventually would, and we buried him on a gently sloping hill beside a large tree. The next day we went back to the cemetery, and the grandchildren all picked flowers off the multi-colored sprays that covered the wet, freshly turned earth.

"Daddy, I'm going to miss Papaw," Bozo repeated.

I know, son. We all will.

(October 15, 1982)

35

Everything's a collector's item

Nothing can provide the incentive to clean up a house like the simple little phrase, "Company's coming."

Better Half and I carried out our own D-Day (D for Discard) operation over the weekend. Relatives were coming up from Houston, and they'd be staying in the front bedroom (which doubles as our "catch-all" room).

Now, don't get the idea we aren't neat people. The trouble is, we're packrats. Nothing — and I mean nothing — ever gets thrown away at our house because everything is a "collector's item."

Tackling the bedroom closet first, I began tossing junk into a trash bag. I was making some pretty good progress, too, until I started to dump a bunch of old letters.

"Stop!" Better Half yelled. "What are you doing?!"

I paused to consider which of the Ten Commandments I was obviously breaking, but after going down the list I still couldn't determine the sin. "What's the matter?" I asked, knowing I'd get an answer.

"Those are the letters you sent me from Vietnam," Better Half said with a how-dare-you look on her face. "They're all here." And they were. There must have been 100 of them.

"And look here!" she continued as she reached into the bag. "Here's the check to the hotel where we stayed on our wedding night. And my corsage from the homecoming dance at college. And ..."

"Enough already!" I said, still digging into the dark recesses of the cluttered closet. "That's ancient history. Absolutely worthless." I knew that was the wrong thing to say when Better Half started crying (My wife is a very sentimental sort. She once cried during an old episode of "Wagon Train." I think it was when Ward Bond's horse died).

"OK," she replied through her tears. "If that's the way you want it, then we'll get rid of some of your stuff, too. How about those golf clubs you haven't used in years? And your Three Stooges membership card? Or the 9,000 baseball cards you keep in that suitcase? Or maybe that shrunken old moth-eaten sweater?"

"It didn't shrink," I retorted. "I got it for playing football at South Ward Elementary, and it's the only athletic letter I ever won."

Sensing I was losing control, I quickly turned to continue digging ... until I found a small envelope. Opening it, I paused for a moment while I contemplated my find.

Toenails.

"They're from the first time I ever trimmed Bozo's nails," Better Half said matter of factly. "And the first Band-Aid he ever wore is in there, too."

And so it was. More letters. The sugar sack we shared on our first date (I took her to a Burger Chef). A 1971 calendar ("It was the first calendar we had hanging in our first little apartment," Better Half said). Old telephone books. All were "collector's items."

I was a beaten man. "OK. I suppose it'd just be easier to add a room onto the house. It shouldn't cost more than $10,000, right?"

"That's silly," Better Half said. "We just need to make a little better use of the space we already have. We just need to rearrange a few things."

So that's what we did for the next four hours ... rearrange. And I'll have to admit the front bedroom hasn't looked this good in years. The closet is nice and neat, and we're all ready for our company now.

But I just hope they don't look under the bed.

(May 8, 1979)

36

Enough camping to last a lifetime

Some friends just returned from a camping trip to Colorado, and they say they had a wonderful time backpacking and sleeping under the stars.

I'll take their word for it.

To be honest, I've never been much on tromping through the woods, and tents just make me tense. I'm sure camping is just great for some people, but my idea of roughing it is discovering the ice machine is empty at the Holiday Inn.

But wouldn't you know it. Better Half is just itching (as in poison ivy) for us to go on our own camping trip. "Think of it. Camping out under the moon, a gentle breeze blowing, the glow of a soft campfire," she said. "It sounds romantic, doesn't it?"

Actually, the last time I slept in a tent was a decade ago when our Army basic training company went on bivouac. And spending three nights under canvas with a chainsmoker named Dale really isn't my idea of excitement.

Oh sure, I'd camped out as a youngster. I remember pitching a tent in the backyard when I was eight. It rained.

It rained during bivouac, too. I mean, it came a real frog-strangler. But at least the rain took my mind off the mosquitoes, chiggers and blisters caused by the 20-mile hike to the bivouac area, located in the heart of beautiful Fort Polk. The 20 miles was what our drill instructor called "only a short military distance — just over a few hills and valleys."

Reaching the bivouac spot in the heart of an insect-infested pine thicket, we set about putting up our tents and digging pit latrines (which was really the pits).

By day we marched around Fort Polk, known fondly by recruits as "The Armpit of America," and practiced maneuvers and read from our Basic Combat Training handbook. I recall the handbook was just chock full of useful military thinking ("In case of nuclear attack," it warned, "remain calm.").

By night, we played war games and shot off blanks at each other (just like we did when we were 8 years old, come to think of it). But I must say I did get something out of bivouac. I got ticks, trenchfoot and an allergy attack.

Ever since that humid July week in central Louisiana 10 years ago, camp has been a four-letter word to me. I decided then and there that "hike" and "hut, two, three, four" should be terms that are only associated with football.

Having survived that experience, Better Half now tells me she'd like for me to suffer through it again. "I'm sure the children would love it," she said as I conjured up images of being molested by a brown bear in some national park somewhere.

By the way, Better Half is an experienced camper herself. Back in junior high she camped out in Idaho for a whole week at a Girl Scout Roundup. She hasn't been quite right since.

But I can already see the handwriting on the wall. I might as well start gathering up the equipment since Better Half wants to go and she's already got the kids on her side ("Gee, Daddy," said Bozo, "We can play army!" I wish he hadn't said that.).

My family has heard the call of the wild.

"Now admit it," Better Half said. "Wouldn't you just love to go out and pitch a tent?"

I sure would. Just as far as I could.

(August 12, 1981)

37

How my ancestor saved Davy Crockett

This is the story of how my ancestor saved — well, at least prolonged — the life of Davy Crockett in 1836 and forever changed the course of Texas and United States history.

Actually, that might be overstating the importance of the incident just a bit. But it does make for an interesting tale.

The story is told in James Atkins Shackford's 1956 book "David Crockett," reprinted for the 200th anniversary of the frontiersman's birth (his birthday is Aug. 17, by the way).

As you probably recall, Crockett headed for Texas after losing a Tennessee congressional race. Crossing the Red River, Crockett and his party passed through the Clarksville area of Northeast Texas in early 1836. There they paused on their journey to stay at the farmhouse of William Becknell, who had gained fame for opening up the Santa Fe Trail in 1821.

While at the Becknells, Crockett decided to go hunting for fresh game, and here's where my ancestor comes in.

According to author Shackford, the following tale was told by one Claude Hall, who in turn had heard it from Pat B. Clark. As a youngster, Clark had heard the Crockett story many times from his grandmother, Isabella Clark. Shackford tells it thusly:

"Mrs. Clark, hearing of Crockett's itinerary and knowing the risk he was incurring, mounted her horse in company with a daughter of Russell Latimer, overtook Crockett and his party on Becknell's Prairie five miles west of Clarksville, warned him of the danger of traveling to the southwest, and prevailed upon him to wait for a guide and recruits to pursue a course bearing towards the east.

"While thus waiting at the Becknell home, Crockett's party went on a hunting trip to the southwest under Henry Stout as guide. The party, when near the headwaters of the Trinity River, met James Clark. Crockett told him of the woman who halted his journey and changed his course.

"This statement called forth from James Clark the remark, 'That was my wife, for no other woman would do a thing like that.' Clark advised the hunting party to turn back, as the Comanches were at that time on the warpath."

Anyway, the Latimer mentioned in Mrs. Clark's story was my great-great-grandfather, Henry Russell Latimer, whose family had settled in the Clarksville area in 1833.

First hearing the tale, I could visualize my great-great-grandpappy's daughter, risking life and limb along with Mrs. Clark, riding through Indian-infested territory to keep an unsuspecting Davy Crockett from getting scalped (Davy wasn't too high on Indians, since his grandparents had been murdered by Cherokees in 1777).

The only problem with the story is that Henry Russell Latimer was 17 and unmarried when Davy Crockett passed through in 1836, and his first child wasn't even born until 1844. So apparently, the storyteller got his Latimers mixed up.

In all probability, the little girl who accompanied Mrs. Clark on her perilous trip belonged to Henry Russell Latimer's brother, my great-great-uncle, Albert H. Latimer. Ol' Albert had three wives — although only one at a time, I understand — and 19 (count 'em!) children. At least five of Albert H.'s 19 offspring were running around Becknell's Prairie in 1836 when Davy Crockett came through, so it could have been any one of them.

Just which one, sadly, is lost to history.

It's fun to speculate what would have happened if Mrs. Clark and the little Latimer girl hadn't warned Davy about the Indians. What if the Injuns had lifted Davy's scalp at Clarksville, and he hadn't gone on to become a national hero with his martyrdom at the Alamo?

Why, Americans might not have rallied to Texas' defense as they did after Crockett's death. Texas might still belong to Mexico.

And goodness knows, Fess Parker would have been out of a job.

(July 29, 1987)

38

A fish story: Matthew, Mark, Luke and John

We are fish-sitting this week, and to be honest we're a little nervous about it.

The neighbors up the street, you see, are on vacation, and they have entrusted us with the life of Fred. Fred is their goldfish.

In all things give thanks, The Good Book says, so I suppose I should be thankful the neighbors don't have a Saint Bernard for us to keep. But if they knew our track record with fish, they'd be a little nervous, too.

It's not that Better Half and I don't like fish. It's just that, well, how do I put this? We have left a trail of dead goldfish behind us.

After all these years, I still haven't gotten over the deaths of Matthew, Mark, Luke and John. That's what I named the four goldfish I won at a South Ward Elementary School carnival. I think I was in the third grade at the time.

They were in a little glass bowl with a wire handle. When we got home from the carnival — after a detour to a store to purchase some fish food — I placed them on our old Capehart TV set and sat there for a long time, watching them swim and blow bubbles.

I remember thinking how hungry they looked, so I decided to feed them. I'd been warned not to feed them too much food, but they were so little and thin and I didn't think it would hurt to empty the whole box into the bowl.

The next morning I awoke and ran into the den, and immediately discovered something fishy was going on. The fish foursome wasn't swimming or blowing bubbles. They were all floating on the top of the water. Alas, Matthew, Mark, Luke and John had expired, and that's the gospel truth. I'm not certain the empty box was the reason for their demise, but it was certainly food for thought.

Better Half, too, had a sad tale to tell about goldfish as we watched Fred swim in his bowl this week, unaware of our violent, although unplanned, history against fish.

Seems she, too, became the proud owner of some goldfish as a young tyke. She was determined to take really good care of the fish, too. She fed them every day and placed pretty colored rocks in the bowl and showed the fish off proudly to her friends.

Her parents took care of changing the water, but one day Better Half decided it was past time to do so. So, without telling her mother, she proceeded to pour out the old water and replace it with scalding water. Death was, as they say, instantaneous. "I thought it had to be good and hot to clean the bowl," she recalled, still shaking her head 30 years after the incident.

It takes a long time for mental scars such as these to heal. Maybe that's why, to this day, we don't own a rod and reel, didn't watch "Flipper" and never went to see "Jaws." Pure guilt.

But now, here we are babysitting another goldfish. And just like decades ago, the first thing we do each morning is run into the den and check on Fred.

Bozo and Bright Eyes have enjoyed watching Fred in his bowl since he moved in. And I'll have to admit we really haven't had any problems with Fred so far (Although Bright Eyes, the 3-year-old, mentioned she'd like to feed him some pizza and a Pepsi the other day. We explained that would probably be a bad idea).

But still, there is the nagging fear in the back of our minds that — just like Matthew, Mark, Luke and John — we'll discover Fred floating on the top of the water.

So we're marking the days until our neighbors return. Meanwhile, Fred seems to be enjoying his vacation, too, and is apparently totally unsuspecting about whose hands his fate has been placed into.

I'd always thought fish were smarter than that, though, considering so many of them spend their time in schools.

(June 27, 1984)

39

There's nothing simple about automobiles

There it was, lying on the floorboard as I got into the car. It was the rearview mirror. And although I'm not exactly what you'd call a shade-tree mechanic, I knew almost immediately the mirror wasn't where it was supposed to be.

Things like this tend to happen to me when it comes to cars.

Either the regulator's irregular or the differential's indifferent or the crankshaft is cranky. It's always something.

And now this. Do you realize how embarrassing it is to have to hold up your rearview mirror in your right hand to see what's behind you? Well, let me tell you, it's embarrassing. Silly looking, too.

I don't deserve this, either, because I try to take good care of my car. I have a very precise maintenance schedule. I check the air in the tires at least once every odd-numbered year and I always make sure the oil's changed during every presidential election. But still I have problems.

OK, so maybe I'm not very mechanically minded when it comes to cars. I'll admit that once, when the engine flooded, I asked Better Half if we should call a plumber (Which just goes to prove you can fuel some of the people all of the time and all of the ... oh, never mind).

For years I thought a tie rod was simply something you hung ties on. And to this day whenever I hear somebody mention a universal joint, I figure they mean McDonald's.

I suspect my not-so-healthy attitude toward the automobile began in early childhood, when my parents bought a pink, and I mean PINK, Oldsmobile station wagon ... with a luggage rack yet. It was a 1956 model as I recall, and it was without a doubt the ugliest car ever built by Detroit.

Oh, it ran great, but nobody ever saw me in it because I'd always hunker down real low in the back seat just in case some of my friends happened to drive by.

Remember when you could actually tell the make of an auto by looking at it? That was before an executive in Michigan had the bright idea of taking those big fins off Cadillacs, and then pretty soon the car looked pretty much like another.

That was back when all the cars were American, when Fords said "Built in Texas by Texans" on the back window and cars were made out of metal instead of plastic.

I'm told cars used to be more fun to drive back in the old days when the crank was located in front of the engine. I don't go back that far, but I do remember when cars were much simpler.

In high school I had a '62 Plymouth with a pushbutton transmission. If you wanted to back up, you punched R. If you wanted to drive it forward, you punched D. See what I mean? Simple.

But simple wasn't good enough. Bench seats got replaced by bucket seats, which would be a good idea except for the fact that not everybody has the same shaped bucket, if you know what I mean.

Then they replaced the spare tire with those tiny spares, the ones that look like they belong on a go-cart. And nowadays cars buzz, beep and, worst yet, even talk to you. I wonder where it'll all end.

Still, it could be worse. We did get the rearview mirror put back in place, and just the other day a fella was telling me his new car had been recalled by the dealer.

Seems there was a defect in his bank account.

(May 10, 1985)

40

So tell me, did Adam have a navel?

Some folks think newspaper people are experts on just about everything.

We aren't, of course, but that doesn't stop customers from calling the newspaper for information on, well, on anything for which they have a question.

Not that we mind, you understand. After all, providing information is our business. And for that reason, newspapers are considered to be a pretty good reference source.

It's funny, but apparently a lot of people never think about calling their public library, where there are people on the staff whose job it is to do research on the public's questions. Folks just pick up the receiver and dial the paper.

Probably the most common request we get in the newsroom here is for the address or phone number of elected officials. And that's one we're ready for. But it's amazing the queries you receive when sitting at the news desk. I mean, there are questions for which you just can't prepare, like the one the other day.

Brrriingggg! "Newsroom. Craddock."

"Excuse me, sir, but did Adam have a navel?"

"Ah, er, I'm sorry," I replied after a slight pause. "I must have a bad connection. I thought you asked me — ha ha — if Adam had a navel." Of course, that was exactly what the caller had asked. And he expected an answer, too, because newspaper people are supposed to know such things.

When it came to being a reference resource, the best I ever saw was the late Ed Leach, the Longview News-Journal's longtime editor in chief. Ed — God rest his soul — was a walking encyclopedia. I mean, he had an answer for everything. And people knew it.

Brrrriingggg! "This is Leach."

"Hey Ed," the caller'd say, "What two presidents were born in Vermont?"

"Arthur and Coolidge," Ed would answer, never hesitating.

"Pardon, sir," a customer would phone, "but can you possibly tell me where to find the name of the first female page in the U.S. House of Representatives?"

"Looper. It was Selda Looper," Ed would respond. "Had blue eyes, too."

Or somebody'd ring up the paper and ask, "Hey, Leach, we got a bet on this one. What'd Roy McMillan hit in 1948 when he played for Tyler in the Lone Star League?"

".307," Ed would answer. "He hit 10 triples that season."

Me? I'm doing well to remember "spring forward, fall back" when people call about daylight-saving time. But Ed Leach — the man was amazing. A walking encyclopedia.

You could ask him to name Charlie Chan's Japanese assistant (Kashimo), the inventor of Lawrence Welk's bubble machine (N.A. Fisher), the number of steps to the top of the Washington Monument (898) or Fred and Wilma Flintstone's home phone number (BC 1234). It made no difference. Ed could tell you.

Not everyone who calls wants information. A number of years ago a woman — you could tell by her voice she was very old — would call the newsroom every day and always ask for the time.

At first I was a little annoyed; after all, we were putting out a paper and I had work to do. But it soon became apparent that the time really wasn't what she needed. She was just lonely. She needed to talk, and she needed someone to listen.

In a soft, faltering voice she'd inquire about the weather or make some other small talk. She seemed like such a nice person, and so lonely. It got to where I actually looked forward to her calls.

But one day the calls stopped. And I never even knew her name.

No, we aren't experts. But it can be pretty interesting working on the news desk of a ...

Brrriingggg!

Excuse me. The phone's ringing.

(June 3, 1987)

41

Man of the road was just passing through

He held the newspaper close to his eyes, so close that the paper was touching his nose.

That's what attracted me to him. That, plus the fact his appearance told me he was a man of the road.

A hobo, some might call him. To others he would be a tramp or a bum. But somehow there was an air of dignity about him.

That was strange, because he stood there in dirty, disheveled clothes. The brown turtleneck shirt was smudged with stains. There was a faint odor of liquor on his breath.

"I have been living in Canada — in Montreal," he said, explaining he had just gotten out of a VA hospital and was now on his way to Houston to see his son. That's why he was passing through Longview.

"I'm going to the Salvation Army to get a pair of glasses. These (he motioned toward his blue eyes) don't see so well anymore," he said, then he stroked his scraggly white beard as beads of perspiration rolled down his forehead from underneath the faded golf cap.

He didn't want a handout. He made that quite clear during our conversation, repeating it three times. He was just in a strange town and he needed somebody to talk to. It was clear not too many people gave him that opportunity. He seemed surprised that somebody — anybody — would listen to him.

"I'm 56 years old," said the Happy Wanderer (He told me his name, but the name's been changed to protect the indigent). He looked at least 20 years older. Years of walking the highways and riding the rails had taken their toll.

"I had to give up the railroads years ago," the Wanderer said.

"Got to where I couldn't hop on a moving car anymore."

He was a well-educated man. He spoke well, choosing his words carefully. People stared at him as they walked by, but he pretended not to notice.

The Wanderer was from a deep East Texas town, and it turned out we'd gone to the same college. That brought a big smile, and he searched his memory for the names of old professors. A couple of the names were familiar to me.

"I also attended the Institute of Paris," he said, adding he was an engineer. It was easy to see he hadn't been involved in any engineering work for a long time, but I believed him. There wasn't any reason not to.

He'd worked at a machine shop in Houston, but one day he left ... "But you know how it is," he said. "Wanderlust, maybe."

He also had been an officer in the Army, and at one time commanded a company of mercenaries fighting in Africa.

"I'm a writer, too, you know," he said. "Short stories mostly. Maybe you've heard of one of my stories?" He named it, and I said no.

"I write like Steinbeck and Hemingway. They lived their stories, you know. Their stories were written from experience. So are mine." He writes his stories down on bags and scraps of paper or whatever else is handy, he said.

What have the years on the road taught him? "Never give a policeman a hard time. No sir. You can't win. If a policeman tells me to move on, I thank him and move on.

"And I run into people all the time who tell me, 'Man, if I want something, I take it.' But I don't have to do that, you see. If I want something, I just ask for it. And do you know what? Most of the time people will give it to me ... People, for the most part, are good."

He apologized for taking up so much of my time and said it was time for him to leave. I asked if he knew where the Salvation Army building was located, and he said he did. "I think I'll stay over tonight," the Wanderer said, looking up at the late afternoon sky. It was cold, and a light mist was falling.

"Wanderlust," he repeated. "Every day is a new awakening. There's always something new under the sun," he said as we shook hands. He pulled the collar of his old tweed coat up around his neck and walked out of my life.

I was glad I'd talked to him.

(Nov. 20, 1980)

42

Violent explosions and tall giants

Once again it's time to stroll down Redundancy Lane, another in my never-ending efforts to banish forever (is that redundant?) such phrases as "viable alternative" and "future plans" and "exact opposite."

I decided to rekindle my campaign to stamp out and/or end redundancy after reading a big city newspaper account about a "violent explosion" that resulted in a "raging fire that completely destroyed" a business.

Personally, I prefer my explosions to be soft and muffled.

Redundancies seem to be popping up more often, it seems. Just in the past week I've read or heard about a "self-confessed killer" in Florida, "hired mercenaries" in El Salvador and the "grave crisis" in Lebanon.

But we come by our redundancies honestly. After all, we learn them at an early age.

Children barely old enough to talk are taught by mom and dad to say "puppy dog" and "kitty cat" and choo-choo train" when a much simpler dog, cat and train would suffice. And youngsters never mention giants or monsters, you'll notice. They're always a "big giant" (there's nothing worse than a short giant) or a "scary monster."

I have my favorites, naturally, and those I have honored with a place in the Craddock Redundancy Hall of Fame. These favorites include:

General public, original founder, free gift (I just hate gifts you have to pay for), agricultural crops, true facts (if they aren't true then they aren't facts. Right?), widow woman, tuna fish, end result, fell down, raise up, deadly poison, revert back.

The sports world seems to come up with more than its share of superfluous words.

During the NBA playoffs, the TV sportscasters marvel over the rebounding abilities of "the tall 7-foot center." It's harder to win away from home, they tell us, because those "road trips" are murder.

Every time Pete Rose (wonder if he has a brother named Repeat) comes to bat, we're told he may set a "new record." While Detroit has been beating every American League team in sight, at one point I read that the Tigers had "won 7 consecutive games in a row."

And every player who swipes second base is described as a "speedy base-stealer" (slow base-stealers are the worst kind).

Here are a few more surplus words I keep running across:

Complete halt, personal friend, present incumbent (this seems to be especially popular during an election year), personal opinion, blazing sun, steady drizzle, ongoing conversation, wealthy millionaire, deboned (as opposed to a boned chicken, of course), few and far between, completely full, badly decomposed (ever heard of goodly decomposed?), ultimate outcome, mutual cooperation, vitally necessary, lone hermit, resupply (the military likes this word, although a simple "supply" would do nicely), hospital facilities, private yacht.

Complete monopoly, unruly mob (I prefer my mob to be restrained and well-mannered), invited guests, notorious gangster, old codger, Rio Grande River, serious danger, pre-dawn darkness (should we then say pre-dusk lightness?), old adage, burned down (or is it more correct to say burned up?).

As you can see, I've probably only scratched the redundancy surface. I haven't even mentioned "pre-board" and "totally committed" and "same difference." And I suppose most folks in these parts also would consider "proud Texan" to be redundant, too.

Anyway, if you think of any redundancies I've left out, you might want to pass them along to me. I could include them in another column.

Or would that just be past history?

(May 2, 1984)

43

Sittin' in the yard a world apart

I used to see them sitting there, but not anymore.

They were two old men, and they lived next door to each other, and almost every time I passed by in my car they were sitting out in their front yards.

They both appeared to be in their 80s, although I'm not sure because I was just driving by. But I do know they were old.

There were probably a couple of reasons I took special note of them. One was because they were always there. Whenever I was driving down that particular street — which was two or three times a week — I'd always look for them. And I'll have to admit there were even a couple of times I went a block or two out of my way just to go down that street to see if they were there. Generally, if the sun was out and it wasn't too cold, they were.

One was a rather large man, with snowy white hair that reminded me of Tip O'Neill. He'd be sitting in a lawn chair, holding a wooden cane and looking out toward the street. The other man was smaller — quite thin, in fact — and he always wore suspenders and would be sitting in a rusted old metal chair.

And that's all they ever did. I never saw them reading a book or checking the yard for crab grass or even taking a snooze. They would just sit there, passing the time of day.

But never with each other, and that's the second reason they made a particular impression on me. Here they were, sitting in their front yards day after day not more than 50 feet from one another, and not once in the two or three years I'd been noticing them did I ever see them talking to each other. It was as though each refused to acknowledge the existence of the other.

Of course, there might have been several reasons for that. Maybe they did talk, and I just drove by at the wrong time. Or maybe it was too much of an effort for one to walk over to the other. Or maybe they'd had a feud, as neighbors tend to do sometimes, and weren't talking to each other. Maybe that was it.

Anyway, I always thought it curious that they didn't speak.

After a while, it got to the point that I even considered stopping and asking them about it. Just pulling over the car and walking up to them and asking them why they didn't talk to each other. But that would be a little too forward, I decided, even for a nosey newspaperman.

A shame, though, because I'll bet they could have really told me some interesting tales. Here they were, long retired, with only memories for companionship, and apparently no one to share them with.

In an age of video games and neutron bombs and locking ourselves in at night, they could have told me about so many things. Maybe one of them had tales to tell about his service in World War I, or could share some long lost tidbit about Longview's past. Goodness knows, they had plenty of time on their hands to talk about a lifetime of successes and sorrows.

But in all the months I passed by, I never saw anyone else at those two houses. No wives, no children, nobody. They were just killing time. Or maybe time was just killing them.

Then one day when I passed by, I saw only the bigger man, the one with the cane, sitting outside. He still sat there, looking at the traffic, but the metal chair in his neighbor's front yard was gone. And I suspected the worst.

It wasn't too long after that when someone started remodeling the house where the smaller man had lived, and after a while I noticed a family had moved in. There were a couple of children there, too. But they didn't seem to converse with the old man next door. And he continued to sit all alone in his front yard.

Well, the weather turned cold, and the old man stopped sitting out front, preferring the warmth of his little house to the winter chill.

That was a couple of months ago, and when the weather began to warm up I figured I'd see him again. But he hasn't been back out in the front yard, and I'm worried about what happened to him, too.

Now I wish I'd stopped the car, but I suspect it's too late.

(January 14, 1983)

44

A last hurrah in the church league

The catcher stands at the plate, clutching the ball tightly and preparing for the impending impact as the runner lowers his head and prepares to throw his body into the catcher.

The two collide ferociously and tumble headlong in a cloud of dust. Tempers flare and an instant later the two men come to blows as the umpires and other players rush in to separate them.

Ah yes, church league softball is alive and well.

Softball is serious business, folks. Some 30 million persons play the game, I'm told, and Longview has more than its share of teams. And let me tell you, it's life and death whenever a team takes the field.

I don't know about the heathens (the open league teams), but a church's honor is at stake every time the ump shouts "Play ball!" for a church league contest.

Now I've played church league softball a number of years, and there's no doubt in my mind that softball is the reason we have so many denominations today.

Centuries ago back in the Holy Land two Hebrew teams got into a squabble, and one of them walked off to form its own team and resulting religion. Then a couple of those got crossways with the other team members and formed something else.

Eventually — all because of softball — along came the Baptists, Methodists, Presbyterians, Lutherans, Mormons, Seventh-Day Adventists (originally known as the Seventh-Inning Adventists) and the others.

You might have heard it differently, but I know the Real Untold Story. Ever since one of the early games was canceled because of rain (when Noah built the ark), religious groups have been battling one another on the field of honor. I'm certain the

Crusades probably started over a softball game.

It's ecumenical warfare every weeknight. "Down with the infidels!" shout the Baptists. "Don't let the zealots score!" cry the Methodists.

And why is the competition so intense?

Well, church league softball is (alas) the end of the line for the players. The last hurrah, if you will. The final blaze of glory for the aging former high school jock. Fifteen or 20 years ago he was the star halfback or centerfielder for ol' Hooter High. He was a superb athlete — and thought he'd always remain one.

But life has played a cruel trick on him. The muscles that once rippled in his chest have slipped into his beer-belly and turned to fat. That once-slim waistline has expanded several inches, and now he has to keep a cap on his head so that bald spot won't get sunburned.

He doesn't cut the handsome figure he did in high school, but that doesn't keep him from trying to recapture his lost youth just one more time.

Now, I never was an athlete. Oh, I grew up in organized baseball. Played about 10 years, in fact. But an athlete I wasn't. I've always played second base, and there's a reason for that. My arm isn't strong enough to throw the ball to first base from any other position.

And hitting? I've often dreamed of pointing my bat toward centerfield — just the way Babe Ruth did that day against Chicago — and socking the ball far out over the light standards. Then doffing my cap slightly to the cheering crowd as I nonchalantly rounded the bases.

But I already know when I go to the plate what's going to happen. If I do get one of my infrequent hits, it's going to be a little blooper that barely makes it out of the infield.

But that doesn't stop me — or the others — from trying. That's why we're all out there playing before family and a few friends. For the glory, as infrequent as it is.

It's a final opportunity to put on that fancy uniform, cap and glove and go out there and pretend we're in the prime of our youth.

Or maybe it's just our second childhood.

(April 25, 1979)

45

Zeb and Pinky's one-track love affair

Zeb and Pinky have had a love affair going for 15 years, and they don't care who knows it.

Zeb is Zeb H. Love, the retired Amtrak conductor from Mineola. Pinky is Pinky Epperson, a professional hand waver from Dallas.

"I love Pinky. She's in her 70s, maybe 80s. It's hard to tell," Love said between sips on his soup while sitting in a hotel restaurant, just a stone's throw from Union Station in downtown Dallas.

Love was in the middle of a coast-to-coast whistle-stop tour as spokesman for the Toys for Tots program, sponsored by the U.S. Marine Corps Reserve.

Since 1947, when Marine Reserve Col. Bill Hendricks started the program in California, 7 million toys have been given to 3.5 million youngsters who might not have had a visit from Santa at Christmas time. Almost 100 children were on hand at Dallas to receive gifts.

On Tuesday, Love was in Texas. Today he's in St. Louis. But back to Pinky.

"Yep, it started about 15 years ago, I guess," said Love. "Pinky — they call her that because she always wears pink — she's lived on Scott Street for at least 65 years. It's about 10 minutes east of town, and her house backs up right to our (railroad) line.

"She'd always be in her back yard waving when we came by," Love said. "And of course, I'd always wave back."

Pinky, a small, frail lady, knew Amtrak's schedule to the minute. She'd be there to wave at the east-bound trains. She'd be there to wave at the west-bound trains. Rain or shine, she'd be there waving.

The waving went on for a long time. Then one day Pinky wrote Amtrak to tell Love she'd baked him a couple of apple pies. She wanted to know if he could stop the train the next time Amtrak came by to pick them up.

Now, as you might imagine, Amtrak officials get more than a little antsy when their trains stop for anything except emergencies (something about schedules, you know). But Love decided this was an emergency.

It took some doing, but Love finally convinced his engineer to stop the train so he could get the pies.

Amtrak officials didn't like it but there wasn't much they could do about it. And from that time on, Love and Pinky would exchange occasional gifts — not to mention waves.

But then Zeb Love retired last December after a 40-year railroad career, and he wasn't there for Pinky to wave at anymore.

When Love's special Toys for Tots train rolled into Dallas Tuesday morning, there was a big ceremony complete with city officials, Marine officers, Dallas Cowboys quarterback Steve Walsh and others.

And guess who was sitting right on the front row with all the dignitaries?

Why, Pinky, of course. Love had seen to that. She was dressed in her best pink outfit, and she was thrilled to be there. She was hugging everybody in sight.

She hugged Zeb Love. She hugged Dallas Mayor Pro Tem John Evans. She hugged Steve Walsh. She hugged Col. Hendricks. She hugged some of the youngsters. She even hugged me.

Later that afternoon, as the Toys for Tots train started to pull away from Union Station, Love reminded everyone aboard to look out the left side of the train about 10 minutes out of town.

"Get ready. Pinky'll be there waving at us," he said, stepping onto the open platform behind the last car of the train.

Sure enough, a little after 4 p.m., Amtrak rolled past Scott Street and there she was.

"Hi, Pinky!" Love yelled, and Pinky waved back, a big grin on her face.

It was, Love said, just like old times.

(October 26, 1989)

46

How the Longview Cannibals got their name

The major league baseball season is winding down — finally — and it looks as though a couple of the division races will go right down to the wire.

But fans in St. Louis, New York, Anaheim and Kansas City aren't any more excited about their teams than the folks in Longview were more than 90 years ago.

It was in the 1890s, on a crisp autumn day at old Mobberly Park, located east of town, when the Longview Cannibals finally earned their nickname.

Before the turn of the century, little Longview was known for two sports. One was horse racing and the other was baseball.

F.T. Rembert, the city's first millionaire, was a horse fancier and he built Rembert Track on the southwestern edge of town. The half-mile oval was located near where the Gregg County Fairgrounds now stand, and the Sport of Kings drew large crowds. The big event of the year came on July 4 when the East Texas Derby was held. Professional jockeys rode the steeds, and thousands of dollars in wagers were made among spectators.

Baseball was the city's other athletic pastime, and Longviewites took their baseball seriously.

The "base ball" club, which had no team nickname at first, played with a changing cast of players. There was no organized schedule, the team playing whenever it could line up a game and arrange transportation for an out-of-town doubleheader.

But whenever Longview crossed bats with Marshall or Tyler or Palestine, a large crowd could be expected. The foul lines were lined with spectators and, just as with the horse racing, betting wasn't uncommon for baseball either. And from the very beginning the Longview team was good.

That particular Gay '90s team was managed by one Bill Maxfield, who had assembled what folks around Longview figured was the best semi-pro outfit in Texas. And the team was proving it, too, going through most of the season undefeated until the day somebody decided Longview ought to play the San Antonio Missionaries.

Now, the Missionaries weren't semi-pro. No sir. Not only was San Antonio a professional club, the Missionaries were actually leading the respected Texas League.

The San Antonio team was scheduled to pass through Longview after one of its Texas League games, so Maxfield arranged for the Missionaries to play the Gregg Countians.

It should have been a one-sided affair, the Texas League-leading pros against a bunch of locals. But Longview had other ideas.

Bill Sherpert took the mound for Longview. He was backed by Billy Alexander, catcher; Will Wilburn, first base; Joe Davis, second base; Jimmy Gibson, shortstop; "Laddy" Leggs, third base; Bob McLain, left field; Frank Whitelock, center field; and Henry Brawrigg, right field.

Sherpert was practically unhittable that day, and lo and behold, David beat Goliath that day. The final score was 7 to 0, and an embarrassed San Antonio nine quickly hightailed it for the Alamo City.

Newspaperman C.B. Cunningham, giving his account of the game, noted that "the Longview Cannibals ate up the San Antonio Missionaries here today."

Cannibals. The fans liked the nickname and it stuck. And for years after that, the Longview team was known as the Cannibals. Longview entered the professional ranks itself in 1923, joining the old East Texas League.

The Cannibals finally went the way of nickel Cokes and Burma Shave signs. But they are still remembered by some long-time residents. And for years, Longviewites fondly recalled that autumn day when the Cannibals "ate up" the Missionaries.

(September 25, 1985)

47

Jogging a spectator sport

Jogging may be the newest national craze, but I'll have to admit I'm not too hot to trot.

"See you later, gotta run" has taken on a whole new meaning nowadays. I've got some friends who are really into jogging, and every year several Longviewites even run in the Boston Marathon.

But I've decided I'm probably much better at running off at the mouth than at the feet. Now, don't get me wrong. I'm not against anybody else running, you understand. It's just that I think I'll watch the rat race from the curb.

Oh, I've considered taking up running a couple of times (once in 1973, I think it was, and again this past Aug. 23), but fortunately the notions passed pretty quickly.

Jogging has had a bad name with me ever since learning about that messenger from Thermopylae dropping dead back in 480 B.C. But I really got running out of my system in the Army, where I was jogging long before it became fashionable. Running several miles in full combat gear isn't my idea of fun.

Why, I didn't even participate in any of those 50-mile hikes President Kennedy made so popular back in the early '60s. Hiking swept the country like wildfire then, but now it's passe and jogging is in. Personally, I think JFK had a better idea when he caused another national craze ... the renewed popularity of the rocking chair.

As my chest slowly sinks onto my stomach, I'm forced to admit I probably ought to take up some sort of exercise program. At least that's what my jogging friends say.

These "Marathon Masochists" have told me time and again how running has given them a better outlook on life, how it helps them unwind after a tough day at the salt mines. Jogging will develop a stronger heart and clearer mind, they say, and the exhilaration they feel as they bounce down the boulevards is, well, exhilarating.

They read all the latest books and magazine articles on the sport and they always speak in hushed, reverent tones whenever they mention the hallowed names of Bill Rodgers or Frank Shorter.

And I can see some advantages to running, even one they haven't mentioned to me yet. If you really got good at jogging, you wouldn't need a car. You could run everywhere. Just think how much money you could save on gasoline.

But then there are the disadvantages, too.

Sore feet, motorists, exhaust fumes, potholes, barking dogs and (even worse) biting dogs. And then there's my body. The typical jogger's attire is a sweatshirt and shorts. Have you ever seen me in shorts? I look like two toothpicks wrapped in a Band-Aid.

Plus I have flat feet. I mean, a tall ant couldn't crawl under them. And in this day and age, when we should be conserving our natural resources, here are all these joggers out getting hot and sweaty. That means extra showers and wasted water.

Like I say, I wouldn't even run for office.

But there's good news for us non-joggers (I figured if I held out long enough, somebody'd come up with a reason not to jog). Recent studies by psychologists indicate some serious joggers actually suffer withdrawal symptoms if they don't get in their daily 5 or 10 miles because of illness, weather, etc.

If they can't get that running "fix," it seems they can become extremely nervous and irritable, even hostile. So I figure I can get hostile without having to sweat.

I'm planning my own exercise program, though, but the only thing I plan to jog will be my memory.

Now then, where did I put that rocking chair?

(October 26, 1979)

48

Remembering Maw

We had promised our little boy we'd take him to the circus, and so we did.

But as we sat under the big top munching popcorn and laughing at the clowns, I was thinking about the events of only a few hours earlier. We had buried my grandmother that morning.

Her name was Abbie, but I never called her that. To me, she was always "Maw."

She was a gentle woman, and she was 85 when she joined her beloved William — my grandfather — in the old Red River County Cemetery.

"I remember the first time I ever saw William," Maw had reminisced a year or so ago. "He was about 12 years old. He had on blue overalls, and he needed a haircut."

As teenagers, Maw invited William to a party one day and served lemonade and tea cakes. He told her right off he didn't care for lemonade. Then there was the time she was babysitting with a little nephew and William came over and asked, "Whose baby is that? It sure is ugly." That sounds like my grandfather. He always had his tongue planted firmly in his cheek.

They were married on a misty Christmas Day in 1917, in the Methodist parsonage. She was 21, he was 23. "I wore a gray wool dress, gray coat with a black fur collar, high top shoes and a rose velvet turban hat," Maw recalled. William, a farmer, wore a blue suit complete with a vest.

His best man came down with pneumonia and couldn't make the wedding. "Didn't anybody hold William up," Maw said. "I held him up." Her parents weren't there, either, because they didn't know about any wedding. A friend informed Maw's mother about the wedding, then asked how it felt to be related to the Latimers of Red River County. Her reply: "Well, we're related to everything else. We won't draw the line there either."

They spent their wedding night across the river in Idabel, at the home of Maw's sister.

And Maw's parents apparently weren't too upset about the wedding, because for a wedding present they gave the young couple a brand new Chalmers automobile. It was black, of course.

The first year was a difficult one. William came down with typhoid fever and was in bed for three months. On top of that, one of the mules died out in the field one day.

But life got easier. William gave up farming, and for many years was city secretary in Clarksville. They had two daughters, and they had each other for 53 years. It was a strong marriage until William's death in 1971.

As a youngster, I spent many a lazy summer day at their Clarksville home, tromping in the woods, playing with their old bird dog Sport, and generally getting my own way as grandchildren usually do.

Maw even saved my life once. I was just a little tyke, sitting in a stroller in the front yard one day when along came a mad dog, foaming at the mouth and all. He was just about to have me for dinner when Maw spotted him and chased him off with a broom. But then, she was always doing nice things for people. It was her nature.

Her health had been deteriorating for several years. Her eyes had long ago grown dim, and the two hearing aids didn't help much anymore. She was checking back into the hospital when her heart finally played out.

So we laid her to rest in the old country cemetery, next to William, surrounded by loved ones both living and long since departed. I'm going to miss her very much.

Oh yes, Maw had a special name for me, too. She called me "Tuggy." Honest, because I sure wouldn't make up anything like that. I was a chubby little baby, and Maw decided I looked like a tugboat. So she took to calling me Tuggy.

She called me that until the day she died, and she was the only person who ever called me by that name.

But then, grandmothers can get away with things like that.

(March 20, 1981)

49

No English questions

"What you studying?" I asked Bozo, the 9-year-old, as he opened a school book at his desk.

"Social studies, Dad," he replied. "Got a test tomorrow."

"Hey, I'll help you study," I said, sitting down next to our third grader. "After all, I was a whiz when it came to social studies."

But Bozo didn't seem impressed.

"Well, Dad, thanks, but it has been a while since you've been in school. And I really do need to start studying now."

But I persisted. "Hey, I can really help. In fact, I've got total recall when it comes to social studies. Education is like riding a bicycle, son. Once you've learned it, you never forget it."

"OK," he said. "If you're so smart, I suppose you could answer all the questions in this chapter. Right?"

"Well, sure," I replied, supremely confident. After all, I thought to myself, it is a third grade test. And just how tough could the questions be on a third grade social studies test?

"All right then," Bozo said, flipping the pages in his book. "Name the seven continents."

"The seven continents, huh? Oh, OK. That's easy enough. There's North America, South America, Europe and Asia. Africa and...uh...let's see." At that point, my mind began to go blank. "Er, ah, oh yeah. Australia! That's six." There followed an embarrassing silence. I was sure there were seven continents when I was in the third grade, but for the life of me I couldn't think of it.

Bozo broke the silence. "Antarctica," he said. I noticed he didn't have to look in the book for the seventh continent. "That's OK, Dad. It's been a while since you were in school. Six out of seven isn't bad. How about this one: What is prime meridian?"

I thought a moment. "Prime Meridian. Prime Meridian. Say! We passed through there on vacation. It's next to Biloxi."

"Wrong," Bozo said, a slight smile on his lips. "Prime meridian is the meridian from which longitude is measured both east and west. It's zero longitude."

"Oh, yeah," I said. "Sure. I knew that. It's all coming back to me now. Right. Prime meridian." This was beginning to get embarrassing. And it was becoming apparent — to both of us — that I didn't remember anything I thought I did about social studies.

It was time to regroup. "Er, I notice you've got your science book out," I said. "Got a test in science, too?"

"Yep. Chapter 7," Bozo said. "Are you as smart in science as you are in social studies, Dad?"

Sounded like a put-down, so I accepted the challenge. "Hit me with your best shot," I said. "I was numero uno in science, too."

"OK. Change from gas to liquid is called what?" Bozo asked.

"Easy, kiddo. Evaporation."

"Nope," he said, again apparently not having to consult the textbook. "The change from a gas to a liquid is called condensation. Evaporation is the change from a liquid to a gas. But I'll give you another chance. Name the three states of matter."

"Three states of matter." Somewhere in the dark recesses of my mind I remembered studying that. But, it had been a quarter of a century ago. I wanted to answer California, New York and Idaho, but I knew that wasn't right. "I, ah, don't recall offhand."

"Liquid, gas and solid," Bozo said. "Those are the three states of matter. I thought sure you'd get that one, Dad." And he grinned a little too much when he said it. Then he tried me again. "What is the measure of how much matter there is in an object?"

I hem-hawed around on that one a while, too, until I had to admit I didn't remember that one either. Bozo quickly informed me that the answer was "mass."

"Oh, sure," I said. "Mass. Well, I don't know too much about mass. I'm Methodist."

By that time I had decided that (a) Youngsters were learning a lot more a lot younger than when I was in school, and(b) it was time for me to beat a hasty retreat.

"But, Dad, I need to study my Spanish, too," Bozo said. "We're supposed to practice the Spanish alphabet and counting to 500. Cero, uno, dos, thres, cuatro, cinco, seis..."

And I'd been given the impression that youngsters only knew two letters of the English alphabet: T and V.

Somehow, I think Mark White and Ross Perot would be proud. (January 17, 1986)

50

A talk with Malcolm Muggeridge

One of the nice things about this job is that you get to meet a lot of interesting folks.

One of the sad things about this job is that some of those interesting folks eventually up and die.

Such is the case with Malcolm Muggeridge, who left this lunatic asylum Wednesday at the age of 87.

That's what the British philosopher called Mother Earth when he came to East Texas in 1979. "It really is a lunatic asylum," he'd said, "and the really serious cases in the universe are sent here."

But then, what else would you expect from someone who had titled his memoirs "Chronicles of Wasted Time"?

Of all the people I've interviewed, I'm pretty sure Muggeridge is the only one who had his figure reposing in a London wax museum.

"Yes, being in a wax museum does have its advantages," he told me that cold March day as we sat in a church parlor. "It makes you very big in the eyes of your grandchildren."

You might not believe this, but Indiana Jones had a pretty dull life compared to Malcolm Muggeridge.

Educated at Cambridge, he'd been editor of the British humor magazine Punch, was Moscow and White House correspondent for London newspapers, served as a British counterintelligence spy during World War II, was a playwright and hosted his own programs on the BBC.

An agnostic-turned-Christian, he became a Roman Catholic at 80.

Whatever the subject, the man with the shock of white hair and that delightful English accent had an opinion on it.

Television ("sleep is one of the great blessings of television").

Pride ("the most appalling pitfall of life").

The U.S. ("Washington has simply handed out money, which has earned them the undying hatred of the nations receiving it").

Sex ("a joke, of course; in fact, it's a joke that gets funnier and funnier the older you get").

Muggeridge told me he'd been fortunate to be a journalist between the world wars. "It was a golden age, really," he said. "To me, journalism is writing and news-gathering, nothing more. I just liked to turn in my copy and hope for the best."

But he said that was no longer possible.

"These new methods, where you are putting your story straight onto a television screen ... well, I couldn't cope with it at all. And now television steals the show. Television has spoiled the business of journalism."

Then he said with a twinkle, "The media are great fun if you don't believe anything they say."

Funny, but we'd also talked about death when he was here.

"You'd be an imbecile at this time of life to still want to accumulate great sums of money or to go chasing after women," he said. "I don't think when I reach the Pearly Gates, I will be asked why I did a certain play or why a contract to write a certain book remained unfulfilled. I think I shall be asked questions of a more exacting nature."

Muggeridge, who had suffered a stroke in August, died Wednesday in an English nursing home. His obituary identified him as "once Britain's best-known media celebrity." It was a description that wouldn't have surprised him.

In 1979, he told me he was concerned because he noticed his figure at the wax museum kept being moved closer to the door.

"I'm afraid I'll find it gone entirely one day, having been melted down to make room for someone else," he said.

But then, Malcolm Muggeridge always could wax nostalgic.

(November 18, 1990)

51

When football came to Longview

The temperature's in triple digits and the humidity feels even higher.

It must be football season.

That annual madness known as Texas high school football officially kicks off this week. One thousand schools will suit up teams tonight and Friday. Fans will dress in school colors and follow their team's every move. There'll be bands and drill teams, pep squads and fancy stadiums — some even with artificial turf.

But it wasn't always like this. Not in the beginning.

The first Texas high school team was in Dallas, in 1900. Nine years later, football found its way to Longview.

Back then, however, folks had enough sense to wait until November to start the season.

Under the headline "FOOT BALL TEAM," the Nov. 4, 1909, Longview Times-Clarion reported the sport had finally come to town:

"Longview, always ahead in the procession, now has a first-class foot ball team composed of the following worthy young men:

"R.E. Rain, J.R. Rainey, W.G. Zeigler, H.H. Watson, Jeff Watson, E.E. Nunsell, Jack Johnston, Ed Newton, Howell Forman, Tully Scott, E.A. Morgan, Earl McCullough, Henry Gunn, Loyd Joslin, Dan Albright, Searcy Birdsong and S.L. Schwartz."

Although active practice had yet to begin, the locals already had issued a challenge to the Marshall team for a game on Thanksgiving Day.

"The challenge has not been accepted thus far, but if the Marshall boys cannot come, a game will be arranged with some other team on that occasion," the paper stated.

While Marshall mulled the invitation, Longview's neophyte football team decided to go ahead and schedule the high school team from Forney, east of Dallas, for its very first contest.

According to the editor of the Forney newspaper, his hometown had "a crack team." But that didn't discourage the Times-Clarion.

"Don't worry about Longview, Brother Robinson, for, after the game shall have been played, your boys will realize that they have 'been up against the real thing'," said the local paper.

As it turned out, the Forney game didn't materialize. The "boys from Marshall" finally accepted Longview's challenge, and the two teams met for the very first time.

The game was a tie.

"On Thanksgiving Day, there was a fine game of foot ball played at Brown's Park between Longview and Marshall, neither team being able to score," a newspaper account stated.

"Marshall had fine team work, being especially strong on ends and backs. Their signals were clear and plays well executed.

"Longview held Marshall from scoring by the might and skill of the back field. Longview has the material for a champion team, but the boys will have to practice and get teamwork.

"This was Longview's first foot ball game and the spectators enjoyed it from start to finish. In fact, it was a good clean game, hotly contested at all times and was anybody's game at any time on play."

At the time, 82 years ago, no one suspected the Longview-Marshall contest would become one of the longest-running high school football rivalries in Texas.

And, I'm sure, no one in 1909 ever suspected high school football would become so popular in the Lone Star State.

Anyway, here's hoping your team has a successful season.

Now, if we could just get the weather to cooperate...

(September 6, 1990)

52

Thank goodness for those coupons

Remember when the three most important words in the English language were, "I love you"?

Well, not anymore. They've been replaced by three others.

"Proof of purchase."

Coupons have taken over the world. Well, at least they've taken over our house. We've got thousands of them stuffed into kitchen cabinets and filing cabinets and coffee tables. I had always known Better Half was a cut-up, but she definitely rates as a world-class coupon clipper.

Now, I never thought that much about coupons — except for the fact they took up so much space, of course — until the other night when I got ready to draw the bathwater and noticed the bathtub was full of plastic mouthwash bottles and peanut butter jars. Having a wonderful grasp of the obvious, I concluded that something wasn't quite right here.

"But don't you understand?" Better Half asked, knowing full well that I didn't. She went on to explain that one of the big discount stores in town was having something called "Triple Coupon Days," and from what I could figure out it was apparently the biggest thing to hit Longview since the Dalton Gang held up the bank in 1894.

"See, the store is going to triple the value of my coupons for mouthwash and peanut butter," she explained. "Then I'm going to send off the labels and proof-of-purchase seals to some place in New Jersey to get an additional rebate. But I've got to soak the labels off the bottles first. Understand?"

I considered telling her to go soak her head so I could take a bath, but that would have been a cutting remark. Besides, 12 years of marriage have made me a much smarter person than that.

"Take this coupon for 25 cents off a can of dog food," she continued (Better Half *always* continues). "Now, I'm not going to waste my time with a dinky little coupon that's only worth a quarter," she said. "Instead, I'm going to wait until they double or triple the value of the coupon before I use it. I'm talking big bucks here."

"But I'm not through yet," she said. "Then I send in for the rebate, which in this case is going to be another 50 cents. It really adds up."

All of a sudden, it began to make cents, er, sense to me. Before I'd thought Better Half was just being frugal for saving all the coupons and cash register receipts and labels on everything from pancake mix to cooking oil.

Well, actually, I hadn't thought of her as frugal. It was more tight than frugal. Oh, what the heck, let's be honest. I'd always thought she was cheap. That's what I'd thought.

With the economy the way it is and folks griping about how expensive everything is, it made me wonder why everybody doesn't take advantage of these coupons and rebate programs. But then, everybody gripes about television, too, and the top-rated programs are still "Three's Company" and "Too Close for Comfort." That says something, but I'm not sure what.

I read somewhere that the average shopper only mails in five rebates a year, so I suppose people just think it's too much trouble.

Anyway, Better Half got back from the store and gave me the breakdown. "I bought $68.62 worth of merchandise, but the triple-value coupons reduced that down to $27.46. And by the time I mail in all the rebates, I figure that'll get it down to about $12. Sixty-eight dollars worth of stuff for twelve bucks. Pretty good, huh?"

Pretty good, nothing. It sounded great to me. Now I understand two very important facts of life. One, the best things in life may be free, but the necessary things in life cost money.

And two, coupons definitely have redeeming value.

(January 21, 1983)

53

Teaching small dog new tricks

It really wasn't my idea.

Bozo and Bright Eyes, the 12- and 8-year olds, decided all on their own it was time to sign up Tiger — that's our Chihuahua — for obedience school. They thought it might even, well, give him a new leash on life.

Now, I don't expect Tiger to bring me my slippers or to fix my coffee in the morning (Heck, that's what wives are for, right?). But I did agree with the kids that it would be nice to have him obey a command at least once in a while.

But when we arrived at the kennel for the first lesson, it was obvious that Tiger was in big trouble. There were seven or eight other dogs in the class, and most of them were enormous. There was a German shepherd, a Boxer, a Rottweiler and most every other big dog you could think of.

One dog in particular, a white one about the size of a small pony, took a special interest in Tiger. The pooch — I believe the owners referred to him as "Mauler" — kept looking at Tiger and licking his chops, like maybe he'd missed supper.

Anyway, our little Mexican hairless — not to mention spineless — got this real nervous look and then jumped into Bozo's lap.

While Tiger kept a watchful eye on Mauler, this first night we had a guest dog — a sort of celebrity canine — in the form of Anvil, a 120-pound Rottweiler who does volunteer work and patient therapy at a local hospital.

You might remember the story the News-Journal's Bruce Hawkins did on Anvil a while back. Once a week he dresses up in a pink smock (Anvil, not Bruce) and carries baskets of goodies to the patients.

As expected, Anvil gave a wonderful demonstration, obeying

every command given. I was hoping Tiger was taking this all in, but when I looked over he was still in Bozo's lap, eyeballing Mauler and scratching behind an ear. It soon became apparent he'd missed Anvil's entire performance.

The instructor had everybody to line up with his dog and the training began. Almost immediately, all of the dogs were patiently walking beside their owners — except for one, that is.

Tiger dug in his back legs and refused to budge, looking for all the world like a miniature mule at the end of his leash. So, as the instructor instructed, Bozo proceeded to drag him by the leash. This went on for several minutes, with Tiger leaving tiny skid marks all the way around the training yard.

For Tiger, obedience school was proving to be a real drag.

Also at this first session, the dogs were to learn the commands of heel, stop and sit. Bozo kept saying "heel, Tiger! heel!" But Tiger didn't heel, and I began to feel like one for even bringing him there.

It occurred to me that Tiger's problem might be that the lesson was in English. After all, he is a Chihuahua, so maybe he only understands Spanish.

But I decided to be positive. Of all the dogs in the class, Tiger was by far and away the best when it came to the command of "stop." He'd plop down and refuse to move, and no amount of coaxing from the kiddoes could get him to cooperate.

When the session was over and we were getting into the car, Bozo said, "Well, Dad, I thought Tiger was doing a little better at the end."

I don't know about Tiger, but Bozo and Bright Eyes did real well. They heeled when the instructor said to heel, and stopped when she said to stop. I was proud of them. But Tiger, well...

Does anybody know where we can get some Spanish lessons, fast?

(July 2, 1989)

54

Paste makes waste

It was useless. There was no way out of it.

"Don't you think we need to change the wallpaper in the dining room," said Better Half. I knew I was in trouble because she didn't really put it in the form of a question. It was more of a declarative sentence.

"Fine, but keep it under $20. And you can put it up," I replied, thinking that was the last I'd hear of that project.

"Remember, I'm into newspaper, not wallpaper."

But wouldn't you know that Better Half, cheapskate that she is, actually found some half-decent wallpaper for $2 a roll? She found a bunch of rolls of discontinued paper with birds and flowers and lots of yellow in it. Actually, I sort of like it, but I'd never tell her that, of course.

Bozo and Bright Eyes had opted for something with Big Bird and Oscar the Grouch on it, but Better Half decided Sesame Street pattern just wouldn't go with a formal dining room.

Well, that was last weekend, and ever since then we've been busier than a one-armed paperhanger. I found out real quick I'd hate to do this sort of thing for a living. Someone who does that all the time probably has, er, too many hangups.

The neighbor behind us hangs paper for a living and she came over and loaned us a bunch of the equipment and hung the first strip for us. "Of course, you know you always hang paper from left to right," she said. Better Half and I nodded, although we really didn't know that at all. Then she said those words I always hate to hear when I'm about to embark on a project. "It's easy. Anybody can do it."

Those are the projects you need to look out for, because they'll do you in every time. "It's easy. Anybody can do it" is the same thing the store clerk told me last year about putting together the swing set in the back yard. I've still got pieces left over from that project.

This being a first-time project, it took us a while to figure out how to match up one strip of paper with another, but we finally got the hang of it. In fact, I'll have to admit the paperhanging went pretty smoothly, even though I was a bit afraid the finished project would look as though it had been done by an inferior decorator.

Of course, we kept wasting paper by mismeasuring and cutting it too short or accidently ripping it. But at $2 a roll, Better Half had bought all the store had in the pattern so we had plenty to spare. After a while we were moving along at a pretty good clip. Slap paste, hang paper. Slap paste, hang paper. The paste tends to get a little messy if you don't watch it. So remember that paste makes waste if you're planning a project like this yourself.

The paperhanging neighbor told us it would take her about an hour to do the dining room, so Better Half and I were pretty proud of ourselves when we finished it up in only two days. That's pretty good for us.

I felt pretty good about getting the project behind us, but now Better Half says she's all fired up to keep going. After all, we've still got plenty of paper left over. She's made a list, see, and next we (I think this includes me, too) are going to do the entry hall. And then the kitchen. And then a bathroom. I can't win.

Hang it all!

(September 15, 1982)

55

Miss Mai still can't go home

Her name was Nguyen Thi Mai, but we just called her Miss Mai.

She had been our secretary in the U.S. Army Command Information office at Long Binh, a few miles north of Saigon, in 1971-72.

And now here she was, on the other end of the line, calling from 17 years ago.

We were a bunch of homesick GIs back then, most just out of school and a couple — like me — recently married. We were working on a newspaper, The Army Reporter, doing stories about body counts in places with strange names: Quang Tri, Chu Lai, Dong Ha.

Being 10,000 miles from loved ones meant it was awfully easy to get down, and Miss Mai did her best to keep our spirits up. I remember how funny she thought my initials were. "You VC. You know, like Viet Cong," she'd laugh.

Then there was the time she'd prepared fish and rice for everybody, smothering it with Nuoc mam, a sort of hot sauce the Vietnamese put on everything. It was, ah, certainly memorable.

Actually, I had heard from Miss Mai once before after coming back to the states. She had called eight, maybe nine years ago, and I had recognized her voice immediately. I did this time, too.

"Were your eyes blinking yesterday? If your eyes blinking, that mean you receive telephone call next day," she said.

It has been more than 14 years since she fled her homeland, since she has seen most of her family. "I left there April 22, 1975," Miss Mai said. Only eight days later, Saigon fell to the Communists.

She was from a well-to-do Saigon family. Her father had been a government official. A brother had escaped with her that day, but the rest of the family ...

"But it is OK," she said. "I be happy now."

Miss Mai has done all right. She lives in California and has a good job, working in assembly at Hughes Aircraft Co.

She said she tries to keep in touch with as many of the servicemen she worked with as possible. She has "three pages full" of names and addresses, she said, from the years she had worked for the Army at Long Binh.

We talked about people from long ago, people I probably wouldn't even recognize now. Goodness, Vietnam seems like a million years ago.

"Have you heard from Glen Rutz? Remember, he was the crazy guy from Missouri. And how about Stu Carlin? Or Lou, the little Italian from New Orleans?" Some she had addresses for while others had simply vanished after leaving Vietnam.

Miss Mai said there is going to be a reunion in Chicago this summer, for the guys who worked in the Command Information office in 1969-70. "They try to get together every five years. I could not make the last one, but I will try to make this one," she said.

I told her I'd round up my addresses of Vietnam buddies, too, and mail them so she could add to her list. We also talked about how nice it'd be to get everybody together from 1971-72.

But that isn't likely to happen, not after 17 years. What was it we'd always said as young soldiers at Long Binh? We couldn't wait until Vietnam had Long Binh forgotten.

It was tough being separated from loved ones half a world away for a year. But when my tour of duty was up, at least I got to go home.

With Miss Mai, however, it was different. Fourteen years later, she still can't go home.

But it is OK," she repeated, her voice growing softer. "I be happy now."

(May 4, 1989)

56

UT owes its finest day to me

Every once in a while, an event occurs that is so big, so important that you'll always remember exactly where you were and what you were doing when it happened:

The day World War II ended. The JFK assassination. Neil Armstrong's first step on the moon. The Great Shootout.

Yes, the Great Shootout. Texas and Arkansas. No. 1 against No. 2. The 1969 battle for the college football championship of the western hemisphere.

And to think I'm the one who made it all possible.

Now, it already has been documented — at least I've written about it here — that I graciously stepped aside as quarterback for Foster Junior High's seventh-grade football team (something about lack of talent, the coach said) so James Street could take over.

I remain convinced that single unselfish act by me paved the way for James to become a great athlete.

He quarterbacked Longview High, then led the University of Texas to 20 consecutive victories, two Cotton Bowl wins and a national championship.

But the game he'll always be remembered for is the Big Shootout.

Saturday's Texas-Arkansas game at Fayetteville marked the 20th anniversary of the Big Shootout, which was voted by sportswriters as "the greatest college football game of the past century."

The setting was perfect. Here, in the 100th year of college football, the top two teams in America were playing on national TV for the championship.

Richard Nixon, the president of the United States, for gosh sakes, flew to Fayetteville to watch the game and award the winning team a championship trophy. Billy Graham gave the pre-game prayer. Even George Bush was there.

Yesterday on TV, there it was for the umpteenth time: That famous film of Street lofting a desperation fourth-down pass of Randy Peschel to keep Texas' drive alive late in the fourth quarter.

It was an all-or-nothing play that hadn't worked all year. When Texas coach Darrell Royal called the play on the sideline, Street headed toward the huddle, then turned back to make sure he'd understood the play selection.

"Coach, are you sure that's the play you want to call?" he asked, and Royal replied rather colorfully that, yes, that was the play.

So Street threw the ball as far as he could and Peschel made a miraculous catch on the Arkansas 13-yard line. The Horns went on to score, coming from behind to win, 15-14.

Texas had been behind 14-0 going into the fourth quarter, but a 42-yard touchdown run by — who else? — James Street put them back in the game.

Street then led Texas to another come-from-behind win over Notre Dame in the Cotton Bowl, but after Arkansas, it was anti-climatic.

He was named Southwest Conference Player of the Year, and the city of Austin even renamed 24th Street for him. James Street Street (I wouldn't make this up, folks) naturally intersected with No. 1 Way.

On Jan. 9, 1970, Longview held James Street Day. A banquet held in his honor had Darrell Royal as main speaker. Most of the Texas players came to town for the event, and the News-Journal published a special tabloid to commemorate it all.

Royal was his usual entertaining self. But while in town, not once did he phone to thank me for stepping aside for James in the seventh grade. The ingrate.

Now, some folks think James was even better at baseball than he was at football. While on the Longhorn baseball team, he threw some no-hitters and even a perfect game as I recall.

In addition to seventh-grade football, I also played Pony League baseball with James. And now that I think about it, I do remember helping him perfect his curve ball.

But that's another column.

(October 22, 1989)

57

Things Queen Elizabeth has never done

"I bet the Queen of England never did that," I said, arriving home from work to find Better Half on her knees cleaning apple juice off the den floor.

"I'll bet she never did a lot of things I've done," replied Better Half. When we started thinking about it, by golly, she was right.

Sure, some folks probably envy Queen Elizabeth II just because she gets to wear that crown and live in big country estates and ride around in that jewel-studded carriage all the time. But if you sit down and think about it, the queen actually lives a pretty dull life. I mean, just think of all the things she's missed out on.

Why, I'll bet Queen Elizabeth has never — not even once — ever put out a Roach Motel in her kitchen. And you can bet your bottom schilling she's never even conducted a garage sale, either, although I'm pretty sure the garage at Buckingham Palace is big enough to have one.

Do you think the Queen of England has ever redeemed a coupon? Driven a carpool? Burned the toast? Of course not.

And just try to picture in your mind Queen Elizabeth, with crown on head and scepter in hand, standing in her kitchen worrying about waxy buildup. No way, Jose.

Kind of sad, isn't it, when you start thinking of all the everyday things in life that she'll never experience. For instance, I'm relatively certain Elizabeth has never:

— Been in K mart.
—Locked her keys in her car and had to hunt up a coathanger.
— Fixed Kool-Aid for the neighborhood kids.
—Had to use the automatic teller machine on Saturday night.
— Popped a wheelie.
— Taken her Instamatic film to Fast Foto.

—Attended a Tupperware party.

—Had to listen for the buzzer on the dryer.

Somehow, it would be hard for me to believe that Queen Elizabeth would, after addressing Parliament, drop off at the grocery store and stand in the express line to buy a pair of pantyhose. And you'll never convince me she has ever even considered using Elmer's Glue, either.

Come to think of it, I'll bet she's never:

—Changed a typewriter ribbon.

—Eaten at a Dairy Queen ("I beg your pardon, but I do not believe I ordered onions on my cheeseburger, young man").

—Used the self-service pump at a gas station.

—Lost a quarter in the soft drink machine.

—Left a note for the milkman.

—Unclogged the sink.

—Worn a pair of Calvin Kleins.

—Squeezed the Charmin.

—Stood in line at the post office.

While her majesty gets to do a lot of traveling and other neat stuff (I suppose being a monarch qualifies her as a social butterfly), it's really sort of depressing when you consider all the restrictions in her life. It's sort of a Never, Never Land, I suppose, meaning she can never do this and never do that because of her station in life. After all, she would never:

—Lick a Green Stamp.

—Pick up aluminum cans from the side of the highway.

—Paint the trim or shutters.

—Clean the toilet bowl.

—Use Mop N' Glow.

—Get shoe polish stuck under her fingernails.

—Drive a truck.

—Use a Weed Eater ("You missed a spot over by the horse stables, dearie").

—Go to town with rollers in her hair.

—Have to wait at home for the cable TV repairman.

—Do the Cotton-Eyed Joe.

See what I mean? Actually, the Queen of England leads a ho-hum life. I bet she has never even taken the Pepsi Challenge.

But that's just as well, because I'm sure she'd just pick Royal Crown Cola anyway.

(June 17, 1983)

58

My opinion of recitals has changed

I attended my first dance recital the other day, and I must say I never knew what I'd missed.

Now, it may seem strange to you that I'm 36 years old ("practically middle-aged," Better Half keeps reminding me) and had never gone to a dance recital. But the explanation is simple.

I was, and for that matter still am, an only child. Growing up, I never had any sisters who took dance, nor did I have any female-type cousins or other relatives who lived close enough for me to go see them perform on stage.

Which was fine with me. Why, as a youngster I wouldn't have been caught dead going to a dance recital.

As every guy in our neighborhood knew, that stuff was for sissies. The closest I ever came to anything that even resembled a recital was watching Annette and her big ears dancing on "The Mickey Mouse Club."

Unless, of course, you count the dance lessons when I was 12. Although you probably won't get them to admit it today, there were hundreds of young men like me who suffered the unspeakable humility of having mothers who forced them to take dance lessons at the local Knights of Columbus hall.

It was bad enough that you had to learn the waltz and fox trot and what we considered to be other outdated dances, but you had to hold a girl (echhh!) while doing it. And if that weren't bad enough, we even had to perform (oh shame! oh horror!) the bunny hop, too.

Fortunately, the lessons didn't last but a few weeks, just long enough for me to get the nickname of "Left Feet" Craddock.

But this was all before I had a 4-year-old daughter taking dance lessons.

Bright Eyes was in the recital the other day, and it was quite a production. There were dozens of children on stage in tutus (some of them were so small I suppose they could more properly be called oneones) doing cartwheels and pirouettes and waving to their folks in the audience.

And there were plenty of folks to wave to, too. There must have been several hundred parents, grandparents, brothers and sisters in the crowded middle school auditorium, and at least half of them brought movie cameras to film the event. I mean, this was a big deal.

And it was clear the youngsters had put a great deal of time and effort into the recital. After all, they'd been practicing for months. Better Half and I had seen Bright Eyes practice her routine to "Deep in the Heart of Texas" so much we knew all the steps by heart.

Funny how having a 4-year-old will change your mind about recitals. There might be a few in the audience who would disagree, but clearly Bright Eyes was the star of the evening. Why, there were even a few times during the "Wooden Shoe Dance" that everybody else on stage was out of step except Bright Eyes. But then, she always was a leader.

Yep, my opinion of dance recitals has changed dramatically since watching Bright Eyes in hers, and I'm already looking forward to next year's production.

I hope she sticks with dance, but with a 4-year-old you never can tell. A few weeks ago she told me she wanted to be a ballerina when she got big.

But during Bible school this week, the children made little paper hats and the teacher wrote on the side what the youngsters wanted to be when they grew up. Asked what she was going to be, Bright Eyes thought a minute, then replied: "A garbage collector."

As I say, you just never know.

(June 7, 1985)

59

Did you hear the one about ...?

OK, I've tried to kick the habit. Honest I have. In fact, it's been weeks since I've done it. But lately I've been feeling myself slipping, and it's finally gotten the better of me.

I held out as long as I could, but against my better judgment (and the advice of others), I'm forced to break down and (gulp!) do another column on puns.

It's not my fault. Really. People just naturally walk up to me and start telling me puns. I don't go out and solicit them. I don't have to, because they always find me first.

Like the story I heard this week about the hungry lion that was prowling the jungle looking for something to eat for lunch. Suddenly he came upon two men sitting beside a tree. One of the men was pounding away on a typewriter while the other was reading a book. Naturally, the lion ignored the first man and gobbled up the second. The reason? Because everyone knows readers digest while writers cramp.

Then there was the tale from a Kilgore College freshman who happened to doze off in English class during a boring lecture about a centuries-old author. The instructor was incensed and threw a book at him. "What was that?" the student asked, rubbing his head where the book had bounced off. "That," replied the instructor, "was a flying Chaucer."

If you want to stop reading now, go ahead. It gets worse.

You also might have heard about the missionary in Africa who was being boiled in a large pot by cannibals. He was philosophical about his situation, however. "Well," he said, "at least they'll get a taste of religion."

I heard this one a while back, and maybe I can remember to tell it correctly. Seems three Indian women were sitting side by side. The first woman was sitting on a goatskin and had a son who weighed 150 pounds. The second, sitting on a deerskin, had a son who weighed 125 pounds. The third Indian, seated on a hippopotamus hide, weighed 275 pounds. So what well-known theorem does all this illustrate?

That the squaw on the hippopotamus is equal to the sons of the squaws on the other two hides.

I warned you.

I believe it was Oliver Wendell Holmes who said, "He who will make a pun will pick a pocket." And that was even before Oliver had ever heard the one about the Internal Revenue Service employee who was telling people to fill out their 1040s on Kleenex tissue since they were going to have to pay through the nose anyway.

Which reminds me that golf is a lot like taxes. You have to drive hard to get to the green only to wind up in the hole.

One of the oldest puns I know was being told, I'm told, back during the days of the Roman Empire. As the story goes, it was during the reign of Nero and two dissatisfied Roman subjects were discussing plans to burn down the city. "I have heard," said one Roman, "that Nero himself is planning to set fire to the city. So why do we not save ourselves all that trouble and just let him do it for us?"

"No, I do not think we should wait on Nero," replied the second Roman. "If we do it ourselves, we can eliminate the fiddle man."

Then there was the fortune teller who sustained a broken arm when she read the Lone Ranger's fortune, and he tried to cross her palm with Silver.

Enough of this already. So in closing, all you pun critics just remember. When puns are outlawed, only outlaws will have puns.

(March 4, 1983)

60

Daughter proves her metal

Bright Eyes is only 9 and she's already into heavy metal. She got braces this week.

That's braces, as in what her father does when he gets the orthodontist's bill.

We began to suspect something was amiss when she went in for regular checkup and the dentist said, "I've got good news and bad news. She doesn't have any cavities, but she's got a $1,500 smile."

"Million-dollar smile, doctor," I corrected. "I believe the expression is million-dollar smile."

"Not in your case," he replied. "I believe your daughter needs braces."

Now, this didn't come as a complete surprise. As a baby, Bright Eyes was a thumb-sucker. Everybody kept telling us she'd need braces one day if we didn't get her to stop (She didn't suck her thumb all the time, of course — just during waking hours). We tried everything, but she wouldn't quit. That thumb was just too good.

Anyway, we made an appointment with the orthodontist, who confirmed that yes, indeed, braces were needed.

"Don't worry, Mr. Craddock," he said. "These braces will force the irregularly aligned teeth to grow into proper occlusion."

"Look, doc," I said, "all I want 'em to do is straighten her teeth."

Now, when you're 9 years old, getting braces is a big deal. Back at school for the first time after getting them, Bright Eyes spent most of the day showing off her mouth to fourth-grade students and teachers.

It didn't take long for her to acquire some gnarly nicknames: "Metal Mouth." "Tin Grin." "Tinsel Tooth."

And leave it to Bozo, her 13-year-old brother, to point out a couple of possible negatives with wearing braces. First, he warned her to avoid thunderstorms at all costs.

"Man, sis, with that mouth full of metal, lightning could zap you just like that!" he said, snapping his fingers for effect.

Then he mentioned the story he'd read — probably in the Enquirer — about the woman in Wisconsin who kept picking up radio stations in her braces. "She had music day and night, month after month. AM and FM. It finally drove her insane and she died," he said, matter-of-factly. "She was Immediate-Top-40ed to death."

Braces were one rite of passage that I missed out on as a youngster. But I do remember when I got my eyeglasses.

I was in the ninth grade when it became apparent I needed help with my vision. Not only was it becoming increasingly difficult to see the words on the blackboard, it was getting harder to see the blackboard.

But I didn't want glasses. "Everybody at school will call me four eyes," I told my parents.

"Don't be silly," said my mom. "They wouldn't do that."

So I had my eyes examined and a week or so later my new glasses arrived.

They had those big thick, black plastic frames with big thick glass lenses that weighed at least two pounds. I looked like Buddy Holly.

To make matters worse, the optician gave me one of those eyeglass cases — you know, the ones that are always stamped with the optician's name, telephone number and office hours.

I remember walking into class that first morning with my new glasses. "Four eyes!" 25 junior high voices rang out in unison. Eventually, of course, I got used to them and so did everybody else.

I'm certain, too, the new will wear off of Bright Eyes' braces. To be sure, she's not exactly thrilled about giving up some of her favorite foods and candies because of the braces. But she says she'll do just what the orthodontist tells her to do, and I have no doubt she will.

Once again, Bright Eyes will, ah, prove her metal.

(Oct. 8, 1989)

61

Lead poisoning is usually fatal

It was 90 years ago this month that Bill Dalton, whose little band of outlaws made a withdrawal from a Longview bank in 1894, was gunned down by Oklahoma lawmen.

And the grandson of the U.S. marshal who may, or may not, have killed ol' Bill way back then has an interesting postscript to the May 23, 1894, bank robbery.

"I had not been aware that Bill Dalton's visit in 1894 is so well remembered in Longview," writes Harrell McCullough of Oklahoma City, who came across an article I had written in June about the holdup.

It was McCullough's grandfather, U.S. Deputy Marshal Selden T. Lindsey, who led a posse to a farmhouse outside Ardmore, Okla., where Bill Dalton was hiding after lifting $2,001 or so from Longview's First National Bank. Dalton bolted from a back window and, according to which story you want to believe, it was either Lindsey or another deputy, Lawson "Loss" Hart, who fired the shot that ended the life of the infamous outlaw on June 8, 1894.

"My grandfather ... shot Bill Dalton through the heart with a .38-56 Winchester. As Dalton fell, Lawson Hart shot him in the back with a .44-40," McCullough says.

You may recall that two other outlaws (another bandit, Jim Wallace, was killed during the bank robbery along with two city residents) escaped Longview with Dalton. They were the Knight (also spelled Nite) brothers, Jim and Bill, and McCullough relates some interesting tidbits about his granddad's attempts to capture them.

"A year after the Longview bank robbery, Grandfather Lindsey located the Knight brothers in the Union Valley of the Guadalupe River in South Texas," McCullough writes. "There he found a man named Beck whose son was riding with the Knights."

Fearing that his son would end up full of lead by hanging out with the Knights, Beck agreed to help Lindsey capture the bandits. According to the plan, Beck would lure the Knights down a certain road where Lindsey would wait in ambush.

"After waiting four days in ambush, Grandfather Lindsey concluded that something had gone wrong and rode through the Union Valley to investigate. On the way he met a funeral procession." At that point, the U.S. marshal learned that Beck had told a Mexican about the plan to capture the Knights. But, McCullough says, "The Mexican betrayed Beck to the Knights who waylaid and shot Beck."

Before he died, however, Beck managed to stay on his horse, which "ran to a house where Beck fell from the saddle. A young woman who was recovering from a severe illness was sitting on the porch. The shock of seeing the bloody Beck fall dead from the saddle was too much, and she died. The funeral procession that Grandfather Lindsey had met was for this woman."

The not-so-good Knights managed to escape to Mexico, McCullough relates, but a few weeks later they returned to the Guadalupe River area with a herd of stolen cattle.

A local sheriff and some cohorts tracked them down and, in a gun battle, wounded one of the Knights while the other brother escaped. "There is a little more to the story," writes McCullough. "Just thought you may find this sequel interesting."

It was in a Menard County gunbattle a couple of years later that the escaped Knight, Bill (also known as Big Asa) died in a hail of bullets.

The last remaining Dalton Gang member, Jim Knight, served time in a Texas prison and was finally paroled in 1914. He moved back to Oklahoma, but apparently didn't learn his lesson.

In 1920, Knight walked into a Tulsa drugstore and attempted to hold it up. The storeowner didn't think very highly of the idea, however, and emptied two revolvers into Knight.

The crime rate in Tulsa went down dramatically right after that.

(August 24, 1984)

62

Today's music weird

The older I get, the more today's rock music strikes a sour chord with me.

When it comes to the music our children listen to, there's a definite generation gap.

I bring this up because Bozo, our 14-year-old, asked my opinion the other day about a song he was playing on his stereo.

He should have known better.

"Like it?" he asked as the song resounded from his vibrating room. He told me it was from a rapper called M.C. Hammer.

It didn't take long before I decided Ballpeen Hammer would have been more appropriate since that's what should have been used on the record, which to me sounded more like labor pains with a beat.

"To be honest," I replied, "it makes me feel like clapping my hands over my ears. Why don't you pitch that tape in the trash can and listen to some real music for a change? May I suggest Beethoven, or maybe Chopin?"

"Now you're talking, Dad!" said Bright Eyes, 10. "I love shopping."

"No, sweetheart," I said. "Not shopping. Chopin. C-H-O-P-I-N. He composed classical music. Or at the very least, you could try some of the music your mom and I listened to when we were in school. Now, that was music."

Bozo and Bright Eyes looked at each other and rolled their eyes.

"I'm serious," I said. "Those were great songs. Not like this stuff today. Songs back then had words, real words. And a real message."

"Yeah, right," said Bozo. "You mean like 'Be-Bop-A-Lula'? Now, that's a song with a message if I ever heard one. Let's see, how did it go?" Then he started to sing:

"Be-bop-a-lula, she's my baby. Be-bop-a-lula, I don't mean maybe. Be-bop-a-lula, she's my baby doll, my baby doll, my baby doll."

"No fair," I said. "We had lots of good songs. You picked one that..."

But Bozo wasn't through.

"Wait. The next line's my favorite," he said, chuckling as he cleared his throat. "She's the gal in the red blue jeans. RED blue jeans?"

Then Bright Eyes chimed in. "Daddy," she smiled, "Wasn't that by the Elderly Brothers?"

"Everly. That's Everly Brothers, sweetheart," I replied. "And besides..."

"Then," said Bozo, "there was 'Who put the Bomp.' That was real popular back then in the dark ages too, wasn't it, Dad? I believe that one went:

"Who put the bomp in the bomp-ba bomp-ba bomp? Who put the ram in the ram-a-lam a-ding-dong? Who put the bop in the bop-sh-bop sh-bop? Who put the dit in the dit, dit, dit, dit-da?"

I was about to give Bozo a snappy comeback, but he started to sing again. This time it was "Tuitti-Fruitti:"

"I got a gal named Sue, she knows just what to do; I got a gal named Sue, she knows just what to do. She rocks to the east, she rocks to the west, she's the gal that I love best! Tuitti-Fruitti, all rooty, Tuitti Fruitti, all rooty, whop-bop-a lu-bop-a-woo-bam-boom."

By this time Bozo and Bright Eyes were rolling on the floor laughing themselves silly.

"OK. OK. You guys laugh all you want," I said. "But I'll tell you one thing. You may have something called Prince, but back in our day we had the King."

"Oh yeah, Daddy," said Bright Eyes, trying to compose herself. Then curling her lip, she bellowed at the top of her lungs:

"You ain't nothing but a hound dog, cryin' all the time..."

OK, so they made their point. Maybe my generation's music wasn't perfect. But I still think the proper pitch for many of today's musical groups is right out the window.

(October 25, 1990)

63

The wall a moving reminder

Have you ever read "Shrapnel in the Heart"?

It's a book by Laura Palmer, and in it are letters and notes left at the National Vietnam Veterans Memorial in Washington, D.C. They are letters from family members to loved ones who died in Southeast Asia.

I picked up "Shrapnel in the Heart" in a bookstore once and started reading, but I had to put it back. It's embarrassing when you start to cry in the middle of a bookstore.

Seeing the "Moving Wall," the half-scale model of the Washington Vietnam Veterans Memorial now at Longview's Teague Park, is a similar experience.

There are 58,175 names on the long, low, V-shaped portable black wall that has been set up beside the park's lake. I'm told that 3,427 of the names belong to Texans.

Viewing row after row of white names on the wall, I was reminded of what Robert E. Lee once said. "It is well that war is so terrible," he said, "lest we grow too fond of it."

I served in Vietnam but had easy duty, working at U.S. Army Headquarters at Long Binh, just north of Saigon. But the "Moving Wall" is a stark reminder that everyone wasn't as lucky as I was.

The names are listed on the wall in chronological order, that is, in the order they died.

To help you find a particular name, books list everyone and show on which panel of the wall the name can be found.

Garland Little is one of the names on the wall and the first one I looked up. Garland was a friend of mine, a classmate at Longview High.

So was Tommy Fyffe. Like me, he attended Kilgore College and took basic training at Fort Polk, La. He died in July 1969.

I found Jimmy Molpus' name on the wall, too. Jimmy was a year ahead of me at LHS and played guard on the football team.

He died in an ambush and was buried on Mother's Day in 1968.

Then there was Bill Northcutt. Bill and I were born only a month apart. He was a Marine private and had been in the war zone just two weeks when he was killed Aug. 23, 1966. I'm 42 years old. Bill was 18 when he died.

I looked up Quinlan Orell's name, too. I've written about him before. I never met Quinlan Orell, but back during the war I wore one of those metal POW/MIA bracelets that had his name on it.

All the bracelet said was "Quinlan Orell, U.S. Naval Commander — Oct. 13, 1968." That was the date he turned up missing in action.

At the wall this week, I found out Quinlan Orell was from Barnesville, Ohio. I'd never known that before.

For a few minutes that morning, I was the only living soul at the wall. Just me and 58,000 names. Then a couple of school buses pulled in and out piled students from a local elementary school.

I think it's good that they came to see the wall. Everyone should see the wall. And maybe, just maybe, we won't ever have to list any of their names on a memorial like this.

Leaving the wall, I have to admit that I was proud of myself. I didn't cry until I got to the parking lot and was sitting in the car.

I couldn't help but think of Garland Little and Tommy Fyffe, Jimmy Molpus and Bill Northcutt, and all the others, and wonder what they might have made of their lives had they lived through that crazy Asian war. But they didn't.

Now they are forever young.

And forever missed.

(October 21, 1990)

64

Go ahead: Laugh

When's the last time you laughed right out loud?

And I don't mean a giggle.

I'm talking about one of those side-splitting, laugh-till-you-hurt, roll-in-the-floor belly laughs.

I thought so. Well, that's too long.

Have you noticed that people just don't seem to laugh as much as they used to? Goodness knows we could have used some humor during the elections (jokes are OK as long as you don't elect any of them.)

Since we need more laughter in this country, I propose that our government create a new cabinet-level position I would call the Secretary of Humor.

In days of old there was a similar position, the court jester. The jester would tell jokes and do pratfalls and generally try to keep the king in a good mood. That way, his highness wouldn't decide on the spur of the moment to declare a war or start beheading folks.

The Secretary of Humor would function much as a court jester did.

Whenever the cabinet got bogged down in a serious discussion about the budget deficit or toxic waste, the Secretary of Humor could say, "You know, Mr. President, that reminds me of a joke I heard the other day."

The Secretary of Humor would tell a joke and the president and the cabinet members would laugh. They'd cheer up and, in turn, would pass the story along to aides and members of congress.

Pretty soon everybody'd be in a better mood. Inflation would deflate, the Gross National Product wouldn't be so gross and there wouldn't be all this gloom and doom talk about recession.

We might even create an annual humor holiday. Patterned after the Great American Smokeout, we could call it the Great American Jokeout.

What makes people laugh, of course, is purely a matter of choice.

To me — and I've said this before — Don Knotts is the funniest man in the world. He may not do a thing for you, but to me he's knee-slapping funny. When ol' Barn walks through the Mayberry courthouse doors, I start laughing. I can't help it.

You might say Don ties me in Knotts. OK, so maybe you wouldn't.

Red Skelton always made me laugh, too. Remember Skelton's old TV character "Freddie the Freeloader," the hobo who never spoke? All of Freddie's routines were done in pantomime. They wouldn't play very well on radio, but on TV they were a riot.

It was a gentle humor and — this was the best part — they were laughs that didn't hurt anybody. After all, that's what genuine humor is. It points out the weakness of humanity but doesn't show contempt. It leaves no sting.

A good laugh is the best medicine, whether you're sick or not.

However, somewhere along the way, somebody decided humor needed to be relevant. Social humor, we call it.

So nowadays we have Eddie Murphy and Roseanne Barr and Andrew Dice Clay telling jokes about the homeless and sex and ethnic groups. Real funny stuff.

I'm afraid we're in danger of losing our national sense of humor, and that's no laughing matter. That's why we need that Secretary of Humor.

She's going to kill me for telling this, but Bright Eyes, our 10-year-old, does the best "Heartbreak Hotel" Elvis imitation you ever saw. She curls her lip and shakes her hips and swings her arm, just like Elvis, and it breaks me up.

It always makes my day.

Funny, but I've found that the worst days I have are always the ones in which I didn't laugh.

(November 15, 1990)

65

My dad and Elvis

Valentine's Day should be a day for memories, so I'd like to tell you what I remember about the day my dad almost ended Elvis Presley's career.

Watching ABC's "Elvis!" Sunday night reminded me of the time Elvis met my pop ... and it wasn't on the friendliest of terms.

The time was, as my dad recalls it, along about 1953 or 1954. Now this was in the pre-"Hound Dog" days before the Colonel had discovered the former Memphis truck driver ... the days when Elvis was playing the Reo Palm Isle, area VFW halls and honky tonks.

My dad was sitting in the Green Hut Cafe in Gladewater one day, drinking a cup of coffee and minding his own business (as he tells it) when Elvis and a couple of his buddies came in and sat down in a booth next to him.

It wasn't long after that someone in the booth — my dad says he's pretty sure it was Elvis — made a less-than-flattering comment about my dad's bald head. Something about the reflection blinding their eyes, etc.

Let me quickly point out right here that my dad isn't bald. It's just that he has a receding hairline that starts somewhere around the back of his head. Anyway, he was a might sensitive about his "thinning" hair 25 years ago, and didn't take too kindly to the comment.

He got up, leaned over the booth and inquired of the trio, "Which one of you fine gentlemen (or words to that effect) made the comment about a bald head? I'd like to know because I plan on making sure you don't make anymore remarks like that."

As he spoke, he grabbed up Elvis' guitar (Elvis apparently carried the guitar everywhere with him, which no doubt explains why he was so high strung) as though he were going to record a smash hit of his own. Besides, my dad wasn't too impressed with rock 'n' roll anyway. His tastes ran more toward Hank Williams.

Well, Elvis looked at his buddies, his buddies looked back at him, then they all looked at my dad, who was looking back at them. Elvis had a sort of "Don't Be Cruel" look on his face while his friends were "All Shook Up." In short, there was a "Whole Lot O' Shakin'" going on.

Let me digress for a moment to explain that my dad most probably could have ended Elvis' career right then and there. Dad was quite an amateur boxer in his youth, and fashioned a 29-1 record as a featherweight before hanging up his gloves for good.

The one fight he lost came at Fort Sill, Okla. He fought a fellow named Muncell, I believe the name was, and the guy several years later became one of the top-ranking pro welterweights in the world. Dad says he had the guy going in the first round ... that is, until his head made a hard uppercut right into Muncell's glove. The fight was stopped shortly thereafter because he couldn't see for all the blood in his eyes. It must have been quite a punch, because to this day he still carries two scars above his left eye.

But back to the cafe. There was Dad, holding Elvis' guitar (and the singer's fate) in his hands. Can you imagine what would have happened to Elvis' career if he'd popped him in the mouth?

Somehow, Elvis singing "Love Me Tender" with a lisp would come across as unappealing. "Wov Me Tender, Wov Me Twue" just wouldn't be the same.

Had he hit Elvis, Kurt Russell (who played the singer in the Sunday movie) and a couple hundred Elvis imitators would be out of work right now ... plus the fact that about 600,000,000 records probably wouldn't have been sold.

Fortunately, the incident had a happy ending. An apology was forthcoming, my dad handed the guitar back to Elvis and he sat back down. Shortly thereafter the trio departed the Green Hut, never to enter my dad's life again.

Dad had held his temper, and thus changed the course of music history forever. For this, I salute him with two "do-wah-wahs" and a "shoobie-doobie."

Besides, if he'd whomped up on Elvis he would have wound up in the Gladewater city pokey. And I just can't picture my dad sitting on a jail cell bunk singing "Jailhouse Rock."

(February 14, 1979)